Next Door
SAVIOR

Also by Max Lucado

INSPIRATIONAL
3:16
A Gentle Thunder
A Love Worth Giving
And the Angels Were Silent
Cast of Characters
Come Thirsty
Cure for the Common Life
Every Day Deserves a Chance
Facing Your Giants
God Came Near
He Chose the Nails
He Still Moves Stones
In the Eye of the Storm
In the Grip of Grace
It's Not About Me
Just Like Jesus
No Wonder They Call Him
  the Savior
On the Anvil
Six Hours One Friday
The Applause of Heaven
The Great House of God
Traveling Light
When Christ Comes
When God Whispers Your Name

CHILDREN'S BOOKS
A Hat for Ivan
All You Ever Need
Because I Love You
Best of All
Coming Home
He Chose You
Hermie, a Common Caterpillar
Hermie and Friends Bible
If Only I Had a Green Nose
Jacob's Gift
Just in Case You Ever Wonder
Just Like Jesus (for teens)
Just the Way You Are
Milo, the Mantis Who
  Wouldn't Pray
Next Door Savior (for teens)
Punchinello and the Most
  Marvelous Gift
Small Gifts in God's Hands
Stanley the Stinkbug

Tell Me the Secrets
Tell Me the Story
The Crippled Lamb
The Oak Inside the Acorn
The Way Home
With You All the Way
You Are Mine
You Are Special
Your Special Gift

GIFT BOOKS
A Heart Like Jesus
Everyday Blessings
For These Tough Times
God's Mirror
God's Promises for You
God Thinks You're Wonderful
Grace for the Moment, Vol. I & II
Grace for the Moment Journal
In the Beginning
Just for You
Just Like Jesus Devotional
Let the Journey Begin
Max on Life Series
Mocha with Max
One Incredible Moment
Safe in the Shepherd's Arms
Shaped by God
The Cross
The Gift for All People
The Greatest Moments
Traveling Light for Mothers
Traveling Light Journal
Turn
Walking with the Savior
You: God's Brand-New Idea!

FICTION
An Angel's Story
The Christmas Candle
The Christmas Child

BIBLES (GENERAL EDITOR)
He Did This Just for You
  (New Testament)
The Devotional Bible
Grace for the Moment Daily Bible

Next Door SAVIOR

MAX LUCADO

THOMAS NELSON
Since 1798

NASHVILLE DALLAS MEXICO CITY RIO DE JANEIRO BEIJING

Published in Nashville, Tennessee, by Thomas Nelson. Thomas Nelson is a registered trademark of Thomas Nelson, Inc.

Thomas Nelson, Inc., titles may be purchased in bulk for educational, business, fund-raising, or sales promotional use. For information, please e-mail SpecialMarkets@ThomasNelson.com.

All Scripture quotations, unless otherwise indicated, are taken from the New American Standard Bible, © 1960, 1977, 1995 by the Lockman Foundation. Other Scripture references are from the following sources: The Amplified Bible (AMP). Old Testament, © 1965, 1987 by the Zondervan Corporation. The Amplified New Testament, © 1954, 1958, 1987 by the Lockman Foundation. The Contemporary English Version (CEV) © 1991 by the American Bible Society. Used by permission. The Good News Bible: The Bible in Today's English Version (TEV) © 1976, 1992 by the American Bible Society. The King James Version of the Bible (KJV). The Message (MSG), © 1993. Used by permission of NavPress Publishing Group. The New Century Version®. © 2005 by Thomas Nelson, Inc. Used by permission. All rights reserved. The Holy Bible, New International Version (NIV). © 1973, 1978, 1984, International Bible Society. Used by permission of Zondervan Bible Publishers. The New King James Version® (NKJV), © 1979, 1980, 1982, Thomas Nelson, Inc., Publishers. The Holy Bible, New Living Translation (NLT), © 1996. Used by permission of Tyndale House Publishers, Inc., Wheaton, Illinois 60189. All rights reserved. The New Revised Standard Version Bible (NRSV), © 1989 by the Division of Christian Education of the National Council of the Churches of Christ in the USA. J. B. Phillips: The New Testament in Modern English, Revised Edition (PHILLIPS). © J. B. Phillips 1958, 1960, 1972. Used by permission of Macmillan Publishing Co., Inc. The Revised Standard Version of the Bible (RSV), © 1946, 1952, 1971 by the Division of Christian Education of the National Council of the Churches of Christ in the USA. The Living Bible (TLB), © 1971 by Tyndale House Publishers, Wheaton, Ill. Used by permission.

ISBN 978-0-8499-2149-0 (Special Edition)

The Library of Congress has cataloged the earlier edition as follows:

Lucado, Max.
    Next door Savior / by Max Lucado.
        p. cm.
    Includes bibliographical references.
    ISBN 978-0-8499-1336-5 (tp)
    ISBN 978-0-8499-1760-8 (hc)
    1. Christian life. 2. Jesus Christ—Person and offices. I. Title.
BV4501.3.L85 2003
232—dc21   2003008090

Printed in the United States of America

09 10 11 12 13 QW 5 4 3 2 1

Will God really live on earth among people?

——*Solomon*
2 Chronicles 6:18 NLT

For Billy Graham

My voice is among the chorus of grateful millions.
Thank you for your words.
Thank you for your life.

Contents

PART TWO
NO PLACE HE WON'T GO

Acknowledgments

I 'm giving rambunctious standing ovations to

Liz Heaney and Karen Hill—for clearing junk, tolerating the funks, and doing the work. I can't thank you enough.

Steve and Cheryl Green—for long-term planning, gate guarding, and being the best friends imaginable.

Susan Perry—for bringing joy—and food—into our world.

The Oak Hills Church family—for sending showers of encouragement and a flood of prayer.

Laura Kendall and Carol Bartley—Your editing and insights are X-Acto-knife sharp.

Steve Halliday—Your study guides always help people dig deeper.

Thomas Nelson—for seeing so much more than I ever see. You're the best!

The UpWords team—for your tireless, behind-the-scenes work.

Bill Hybels—Thanks for sharing the secret of Matthew. Thanks even more for living it.

Charles Prince—for jewels of knowledge and a treasure chest of kindness.

Todd Phillips—Thanks for your timely insights and appreciated encouragement.

Larry King and team—Thanks for the seed thoughts.

Michael W., 3D, and the CTAW group—What a ride! Thanks for listening to these messages.

My Jenna, Andrea, and Sara—Should I ever doubt God's goodness, I need only to look at you. Thanks for being the best daughters in the world.

Acknowledgments

My wife, Denalyn—If love were a mountain, then my love for you would be the Alps. I'll love you forever.

You, the reader—May you find safe living in his neighborhood.

And you, dear Jesus—Eternal thanks for moving in.

I

Our Next Door Savior

Now when Jesus came into the district of Caesarea Philippi, He was asking His disciples, "Who do people say that the Son of Man is?" And they said, "Some say John the Baptist; and others, Elijah; but still others, Jeremiah, or one of the prophets." He said to them, "But who do you say that I am?" Simon Peter answered, "You are the Christ, the Son of the living God."

Matthew 16:13–16

The words hang in the air like a just-rung bell. "Who do you say that I am?" Silence settles on the horseshoe of followers. Nathanael clears his throat. Andrew ducks his eyes. John chews on a fingernail. Judas splits a blade of grass. He won't speak up. Never does. Peter will. Always does.

But he pauses first. Jesus' question is not new to him.

The previous thousand times, however, Peter had kept the question to himself.

That day in Nain? He'd asked it. Most people stand quietly as funeral processions pass. Mouths closed. Hands folded. Reverently silent. Not Jesus. He approached the mother of the dead boy and whispered something in her ear that made her turn and look at her son. She started to object but didn't. Signaling to the pallbearers, she instructed, "Wait."

Jesus walked toward the boy. Eye level with the corpse, he spoke. Not over it, as a prayer, but to it, as a command. "Young man, I say to you, arise!" (Luke 7:14).

With the tone of a teacher telling students to sit or the authority of a mom telling kids to get out of the rain, Jesus commanded the dead boy *not to be dead.* And the boy obeyed. Cold skin warmed. Stiff limbs moved. White cheeks flushed. The men lowered the coffin, and the boy jumped up and into his mother's arms. Jesus "gave him back to his mother" (Luke 7:15).

An hour later Jesus and the guys were eating the evening meal. He laughed at a joke and asked for seconds on bread, and the irony of it all jolted Peter. *Who are you?* he wondered so softly that no one but God could hear. *You just awakened the dead! Should you not be encased in light or encircled by angels or enthroned higher than a thousand Caesars? Yet, look at you—wearing clothes I would wear and laughing at jokes I tell and eating the food we all eat. Is this what death defeaters do? Just who are you?*

3

And then there was the storm. The tie-yourself-to-the-mast-and-kiss-your-boat-good-bye storm. Ten-foot waves yanked the disciples first forward and then backward, leaving the boat ankle-deep in water. Matthew's face blanched to the shade of spaetzle. Thomas death-gripped the stern. Peter suggested that they pray the Lord's Prayer. Better still, that the Lord lead them in the Lord's Prayer. That's when he heard the Lord.

Snoring.

Jesus was asleep. Back against the bow. Head drooped forward. Chin flopping on sternum as the hull bounced on waves. "Jesus!" Peter shouted.

The carpenter woke up, looked up. He wiped the rain from his eyes, puffed both cheeks with a sigh, and stood. He raised first his hand, then his voice, and as fast as you could say "glassy," the water became just that. Jesus smiled and sat, and Peter stared and wondered, "Who is this? Even the wind and the waves obey him!" (Mark 4:41 NCV).

This time Jesus is the one posing the question: "Who do you say that I am?" (Matt. 16:15).

Perhaps Peter's reply had the tone of an anchorman on the six o'clock news. Arched eyebrow. Half smile. James Bondish baritone voice. "I believe that you are the Son of God." But I doubt it.

I'm seeing Peter kick the dirt a bit. Clear his throat. Less swagger, more swallow. Gulp. More like a first-time parachutist about to jump out of the plane. "Are you ready to jump?" he's asked. "I, uh, I, uh, I, uh . . ."

"Who do you say that I am?"

"I, uh, I, uh . . . I believe . . . that you are the Christ, the Son of the living God" (see Matt. 16:16).

If Peter was hesitant, you can hardly fault him. How many times do you call a callous-handed nail bender from a one-camel town the Son of God?

There was something wrong with the picture.

We used to look at such scenes in elementary school. To keep us occupied, the teacher would pass out drawings with the question at the bottom "What's wrong with this picture?" Remember them? We'd look closely for something that didn't fit. A farmyard scene with a piano near the water trough. A classroom with a pirate seated on the back row. An astronaut on the moon with a pay phone in the background. We'd ponder the picture and point to the piano or pirate or pay phone and say, "This doesn't fit." Something is out of place. Something is absurd. Pianos don't belong in farmyards. Pirates don't sit

in classrooms. Pay phones aren't found on the moon, and God doesn't chum with the common folk or snooze in fishing boats.

But according to the Bible he did. "For in Christ there is all of God in a human body" (Col. 2:9 TLB). Jesus was not a godlike man, nor a manlike God. He was God-man.

Midwifed by a carpenter.

Bathed by a peasant girl.

The maker of the world with a bellybutton.

The author of the Torah being taught the Torah.

Heaven's human. And because he was, we are left with scratch-your-head, double-blink, what's-wrong-with-this-picture? moments like these:

Bordeaux instead of H_2O.

A cripple sponsoring the town dance.

A sack lunch satisfying five thousand tummies.

And, most of all, a grave: guarded by soldiers, sealed by a rock, yet vacated by a three-days-dead man.

What do we do with such moments?

What do we do with such *person?* We applaud men for doing good things. We enshrine God for doing great things. But when a man does God things?

One thing is certain, we can't ignore him.

Why would we want to? If these moments are factual, if the claim of Christ is actual, then he was, at once, man and God.

There he was, the single most significant person who ever lived. Forget MVP; he is the entire league. The head of the parade? Hardly. No one else shares the street. Who comes close? Humanity's best and brightest fade like dime-store rubies next to him.

Dismiss him? We can't.

Resist him? Equally difficult. Don't we need a God-man Savior? A just-God Jesus could make us but not understand us. A just-man Jesus could love us but never save us. But a God-man Jesus? Near enough to touch. Strong enough to trust. A next door Savior.

A Savior found by millions to be irresistible. Nothing compares to "the surpassing worth of knowing Christ Jesus my Lord" (Phil. 3:8 RSV). The reward of Christianity is Christ.

Do you journey to the Grand Canyon for the souvenir T-shirt or the snow globe with the snowflakes that fall when you shake it? No. The reward of the Grand Canyon is the Grand Canyon. The wide-eyed realization that you are part of something ancient, splendid, powerful, and greater than you.

The cache of Christianity is Christ. Not money in the bank or a car in the garage or a healthy body or a better self-image. Secondary and tertiary fruits perhaps. But the Fort Knox of faith is Christ. Fellowship with him. Walking with him. Pondering him. Exploring him. The heart-stopping realization that in him you are part of something ancient, endless, unstoppable, and unfathomable. And that he, who can dig the Grand Canyon with his pinkie, thinks you're worth his death on Roman timber. Christ is the reward of Christianity. Why else would Paul make him his supreme desire? "I want to know Christ" (Phil. 3:10 NCV).

Do you desire the same? My idea is simple. Let's look at some places he went and some people he touched. Join me on a quest for his "God-manness." You may be amazed.

More important, you may be changed. "We all, with unveiled face, beholding the glory of the Lord, are being changed into his likeness from one degree of glory to another; for this comes from the Lord who is the Spirit" (2 Cor. 3:18 RSV).

As we behold him, we become like him.

I experienced this principle firsthand when an opera singer visited our church. We didn't know his voice was trained. You couldn't have known by his corduroy coat and loafers. No tuxedo, cummerbund, or silk tie. His appearance raised no eyebrow, but his voice certainly did. I should know. He was in the pew behind mine.

His vibrato made dentures rattle and rafters shake. He tried to contain himself. But how can a tuba hide in a room of piccolos?

For a moment I was startled. But within a verse, I was inspired. Emboldened by his volume, I lifted mine. Did I sing better? Not even I could hear me. My warbles were lost in his talent. But did I try harder? No doubt. His power brought out the best in me.

Could your world use a little music? If so, invite heaven's baritone to cut loose. He may look as common as the guy next door, but just wait till you see what he can do. Who knows? A few songs with him might change the way you sing.

Forever.

Part One

NO PERSON HE WON'T TOUCH

M ost of us had a hard time learning to tie our shoes. Squirting tooth-paste on a brush was tough enough, but tightening shoes by wrapping strings together? Nothing easy about that. Besides, who needs them? Wear loafers. Go barefoot. Who came up with the idea of shoes anyhow?

And knees don't help. Always in your face. Leaning around them, pushing them away—a person can't concentrate.

And, oh, the advice! Everyone had a different approach. "Make a tree with the loop, and let the squirrel run around it into the hole." "Shape a rabbit ear, and then wrap it with a ribbon." Dad said, "Go fast." Your uncle said to take your time. Can't anyone agree? Only on one thing. You need to know how.

Learning to tie your shoes is a rite of passage. Right in there with first grade and first bike is first shoe tying. But, oh, how dreadful is the process.

Just when you think you've made the loops and circled the tree . . . you get the rabbit ears in either hand and give them a triumphant yank and, voilà!— a knot. Unbeknownst to you, you've just been inducted into reality.

My friend Roy used to sit on a park bench for a few minutes each morning. He liked to watch the kids gather and play at the bus stop. One day he noticed a little fellow, maybe five or six years of age, struggling to board the bus. While others were climbing on, he was leaning down, frantically trying to disentangle a knotted shoestring. He grew more anxious by the moment, frantic eyes darting back and forth between the shoe and the ride.

All of a sudden it was too late. The door closed.

The boy fell back on his haunches and sighed. That's when he saw Roy. With tear-filled eyes he looked at the man on the bench and asked, "Do you untie knots?"

Jesus loves that request.

Life gets tangled. People mess up. You never outgrow the urge to look up and say, "Help!"

Jesus had a way of appearing at such moments. Peter's empty boat. Nicodemus's empty heart. Matthew has a friend issue. A woman has a health issue. Look who shows up.

Jesus, our next door Savior.

"Do you untie knots?"

"Yes."

2

Christ's Theme Song

Every Person

HEBREWS 2:17–18

M ost families keep their family secrets a secret. Most don't talk about the swindling uncle or the streetwalking great-aunt. Such stories remain unmentioned at the family reunion and unrecorded in the family Bible.

That is unless you are the God-man. Jesus displays the bad apples of his family tree in the first chapter of the New Testament. You've barely dipped a toe into Matthew's gospel when you realize Jesus hails from the Tilted-Halo Society. Rahab was a Jericho harlot. Grandpa Jacob was slippery enough to warrant an electric ankle bracelet. David had a personality as irregular as a Picasso painting—one day writing psalms, another day seducing his captain's wife. But did Jesus erase his name from the list? Not at all.

You'd think he would have. *Entertainment Tonight* could quarry a season of gossip out of these stories. Why did Jesus hang his family's dirty laundry on the neighborhood clothesline?

Because your family has some too. An uncle with a prison record. The dad who never came home. The grandparent who ran away with the coworker. If your family tree has bruised fruit, then Jesus wants you to know, "I've been there."

The phrase "I've been there" is in the chorus of Christ's theme song. To the lonely, Jesus whispers, "I've been there." To the discouraged, Christ nods his head and sighs, "I've been there."

Just look at his hometown. A sleepy, humble, forgotten hamlet.

To find its parallel in our world, where would we go? We'd leave the United States. We'd bypass Europe and most of Latin America. Israel wasn't a superpower or a commercial force or a vacation resort. The land Joshua settled and Jesus loved barely registered on the Roman Empire radar screen!

But it was there. Caesar's soldiers occupied it. Like Poland in the 1940s or Guatemala in the 1980s, the Judean hills knew the rumbles of a foreign army. Though you've got to wonder if Roman soldiers ever made it as far north as Nazareth.

Envision a dusty, quiet village. A place that would cause people to say, "Does anything good come out of _____?" In the case of Christ, the blank was filled with the name Nazareth. An unimpressive town in an unimpressive nation.

Where do we go to find such a place today? Iraq? Afghanistan? Burkina Faso? Cambodia? Take your pick. Find a semiarid, agriculturally based region orbiting on the fringe of any social epicenter. Climb into a jeep, and go there looking for a family like Jesus'.

Ignore the nicer homes of the village. Joseph and Mary celebrated the birth of Jesus with a temple offering of two turtledoves, the gift of the poor (Luke 2:22–24). Go to the poorer part of town. Not poverty stricken or destitute, just simple.

And look for a single mom. The absence of Joseph in the adult life of Jesus suggests that Mary may have raised him and the rest of the kids alone. We need a simple home with a single mom and an ordinary laborer. Jesus' neighbors remembered him as a worker. "He's just a carpenter" (Mark 6:3 MSG).

Jesus had dirty hands, sweat-stained shirts, and—this may surprise you—common looks. "No stately form or majesty that we should look upon Him, nor appearance that we should be attracted to Him" (Isa. 53:2).

Drop-dead smile? Steal-your-breath physique? No. Heads didn't turn when Jesus passed. If he was anything like his peers, he had a broad peasant's face, dark olive skin, short curly hair, and a prominent nose. He stood five feet one inch tall and weighed around 110 pounds.[1] Hardly worthy of a *GQ* cover. According to a third-century historian, Origen, "his body was small and ill-shapen and ignoble."[2]

Are your looks run-of-the-mill and your ways simple? So were his. He's been there.

Questionable pedigree. Raised in an overlooked nation among oppressed people in an obscure village. Simple home. Single mom. An ordinary laborer with ordinary looks. Can you spot him? See the adobe house with the thatched roof? Yes, the one with the chickens in the yard and the gangly teenager repairing chairs in the shed. Word has it he can fix your plumbing as well.

He's been there.

"He had to enter into every detail of human life. Then, when he came before God as high priest to get rid of the people's sins, he would have already experienced it all himself—all the pain, all the testing—and would be able to help where help was needed" (Heb. 2:17–18 MSG).

Are you poor? Jesus knows how you feel. Are you on the lowest rung of the social ladder? He understands. Ever feel taken advantage of? Christ paid taxes to a foreign emperor.

He's been there. He understands the meaning of obscurity.

But what if your life is not obscure? What if you have a business to run or crowds to manage or a classroom to lead? Can Jesus relate?

Absolutely. He recruited and oversaw his own organization. Seventy men plus an assortment of women looked to him for leadership. Do you make budgets and lead meetings and hire personnel? Christ knows leadership is not easy. His group included a zealot who hated the Romans and a tax collector who had worked for them. The mother of his key men demanded special treatment for her sons. Jesus understands the stress of leadership.

Ever feel as if you need to get away? So did Jesus. "Early the next morning, while it was still dark, Jesus woke and left the house. He went to a lonely place, where he prayed" (Mark 1:35 NCV).

Ever have so many demands that you can't stop for lunch? He can relate. "Crowds of people were coming and going so that Jesus and his followers did not even have time to eat" (Mark 6:31 NCV).

Do you have too much e-mail to fit in a screen or too many calls to make in a day? Christ has been there. "Great crowds came to Jesus, bringing with them the lame, the blind, the crippled, those who could not speak, and many others. They put them at Jesus' feet, and he healed them" (Matt. 15:30 NCV).

How about family tension? "When his family heard what was happening, they tried to take him home with them. 'He's out of his mind,' they said" (Mark 3:21 NLT).

Have you been falsely accused? Enemies called Jesus a wino and a chowhound (Matt. 11:19). The night before his death people "tried to find something false against Jesus so they could kill him" (Matt. 26:59 NCV).

Do your friends ever let you down? When Christ needed help, his friends dozed off. "You men could not stay awake with me for one hour?" (Matt. 26:40 NCV).

Unsure of the future? Jesus was. Regarding the last day of history, he explained, "No one knows when that day or time will be, not the angels in heaven, not even the Son" (Matt. 24:36 NCV). Can Jesus be the Son of God and not know something? He can if he chooses not to. Knowing you would face the unknown, he chose to face the same.

Jesus has been there. He experienced "all the pain, all the testing" (Heb. 2:18 MSG). Jesus was angry enough to purge the temple, hungry enough to eat raw grain, distraught enough to weep in public, fun loving enough to be called a drunkard, winsome enough to attract kids, weary enough to sleep in a storm-bounced boat, poor enough to sleep on dirt and borrow a coin for a sermon illustration, radical enough to get kicked out of town, responsible enough to care for his mother, tempted enough to know the smell of Satan, and fearful enough to sweat blood.

But why? Why would heaven's finest Son endure earth's toughest pain? So you would know that "he is able . . . to run to the cry of . . . those who are being tempted and tested and tried" (Heb. 2:18 AMP).

Whatever you are facing, he knows how you feel.

A couple of days ago twenty thousand of us ran through the streets of San Antonio, raising money for breast cancer research. Most of us ran out of kindness, happy to log three miles and donate a few dollars to the cause. A few ran in memory of a loved one, others in honor of a cancer survivor. We ran for different reasons. But no runner was more passionate than one I spotted. A bandanna covered her bald head, and dark circles shadowed her eyes. She had cancer. While we ran out of kindness, she ran out of conviction. She knows how cancer victims feel. She's been there.

So has Jesus. "He is able . . . to run to the cry of . . . those who are being tempted and tested and tried."

When you turn to him *for* help, he runs to you *to* help. Why? He knows how you feel. He's been there.

By the way, remember how Jesus was not reluctant to call his ancestors his family? He's not ashamed of you either: "Jesus, who makes people holy, and those who are made holy are from the same family. So he is not ashamed to call them his brothers and sisters" (Heb. 2:11 NCV).

He's not ashamed of you. Nor is he confused by you. Your actions don't bewilder him. Your tilted halo doesn't trouble him. So go to him. After all, you're a part of his family.

3

Friend of Flops

Shady People
MATTHEW 9:9–13

A s Jesus was going down the road, he saw Matthew sitting at his tax-collection booth. 'Come, be my disciple,' Jesus said to him. So Matthew got up and followed him" (Matt. 9:9 NLT).

The surprise in this invitation is the one invited—a tax collector. Combine the greed of an embezzling executive with the presumption of a hokey television evangelist. Throw in the audacity of an ambulance-chasing lawyer and the cowardice of a drive-by sniper. Stir in a pinch of a pimp's morality, and finish it off with the drug peddler's code of ethics— and what do you have?

A first-century tax collector.

According to the Jews, these guys ranked barely above plankton on the food chain. Caesar permitted these Jewish citizens to tax almost any-thing—your boat, the fish you caught, your house, your crops. As long as Caesar got his due, they could keep the rest.

Matthew was a *public* tax collector. Private tax collectors hired other people to do the dirty work. Public publicans, like Matthew, just pulled their stretch limos into the poor side of town and set up shop. As crooked as corkscrews.

His given name was Levi, a priestly name (Mark 2:14; Luke 5:27–28). Did his parents aspire for him to enter the priesthood? If so, he was a flop in the family circle.

You can bet he was shunned. The neighborhood cookouts? Never invited. High-school reunions? Somehow his name was left off the list. The guy was avoided like streptococcus A. Everybody kept his distance from Matthew.

Everyone except Jesus. "'Come, be my disciple,' Jesus said to him. So Matthew got up and followed him" (Matt. 9:9 NLT).

Matthew must have been ripe. Jesus hardly had to tug. Within a punctuation mark, Matthew's shady friends and Jesus' green followers are swapping e-mail addresses. "Then Levi gave a big dinner for Jesus at his house. Many tax collectors and other people were eating there, too" (Luke 5:29 NCV).

What do you suppose led up to that party? Let's try to imagine. I can see Matthew going back to his office and packing up. He removes the Quisling of the Year Award from the wall and boxes up the Shady Business School certificate. His coworkers start asking questions.

"What's up, Matt? Headed on a cruise?"

"Hey, Matthew, the Missus kick you out?"

Matthew doesn't know what to say. He mumbles something about a job change. But as he reaches the door, he pauses. Holding his box full of office supplies, he looks back. They're giving him hangdog looks—kind of sad, puzzled.

He feels a lump in his throat. Oh, these guys aren't much. Parents warn their kids about this sort. Salty language. Mardi Gras morals. They keep the phone number of the bookie on speed dial. The bouncer at the Gentlemen's Club sends them birthday cards. But a friend is a friend. Yet what can he do? Invite them to meet Jesus? Yeah, right. They like preachers the way sheep like butchers. Tell them to tune in to the religious channel on TV? Then they'd think cotton-candy hair is a requirement for following Christ. What if he snuck little Torah tracts in their desks? Nah, they don't read.

So, not knowing what else to do, he shrugs his shoulders and gives them a nod. "These stupid allergies," he says, rubbing the mist from one eye.

Later that day the same thing happens. He goes to the bar to settle up his account. The décor is blue-collar chic: a seedy, smoky place with a Budweiser chandelier over the pool table and a jukebox in the corner. Not the country club, but for Matthew, it's his home on the way home. And when he tells the owner he's moving on, the bartender responds, "Whoa, Matt. What's comin' down?"

Matthew mumbles an excuse about a transfer but leaves with an empty feeling in his gut.

Later on he meets up with Jesus at a diner and shares his problem. "It's my buddies—you know, the guys at the office. And the fellows at the bar."

"What about them?" Jesus asks.

"Well, we kinda run together, you know. I'm gonna miss 'em. Take Josh for instance—as slick as a can of Quaker State, but he visits orphans on Sunday. And Bruno at the gym? Can crunch you like a roach, but I've never had a better friend. He's posted bail for me three times."

Jesus motions for him to go on. "What's the problem?"

"Well, I'm gonna miss those guys. I mean, I've got nothing against Peter and James and John, Jesus . . . but they're Sunday morning, and I'm Saturday night. I've got my own circle, ya know?"

Jesus starts to smile and shake his head. "Matthew, Matthew, you think I came to quarantine you? Following me doesn't mean forgetting your friends. Just the opposite. I want to meet them."

"Are you serious?"

"Is the high priest a Jew?"

"But, Jesus, these guys . . . half of them are on parole. Josh hasn't worn socks since his Bar Mitzvah . . ."

"I'm not talking about a religious service, Matthew. Let me ask you— what do you like to do? Bowl? Play Monopoly? How's your golf game?"

Matthew's eyes brighten. "You ought to see me cook. I get on steaks like a whale on Jonah."

"Perfect." Jesus smiles. "Then throw a little going-away party. A hang-up-the-clipboard bash. Get the gang together."

Matthew's all over it. Calling the caterer, his housekeeper, his secretary. "Get the word out, Thelma. Drinks and dinner at my house tonight. Tell the guys to come and bring a date."

And so Jesus ends up at Matthew's house, a classy split-level with a view of the Sea of Galilee. Parked out front is everything from BMWs to Harleys to limos. And the crowd inside tells you this is anything but a clergy conference.

Earrings on the guys and tattoos on the girls. Moussified hair. Music that rumbles teeth roots. And buzzing around in the middle of the group is Matthew, making more connections than an electrician. He hooks up Peter with the tax collector bass club and Martha with the kitchen staff. Simon the Zealot meets a high-school debate partner. And Jesus? Beaming. What could be better? Sinners and saints in the same room, and no one's trying to determine who is which. But an hour or so into the evening the door opens, and an icy breeze blows in. "The Pharisees and the men who taught the law for the Pharisees began to complain to Jesus' followers, 'Why do you eat and drink with tax collectors and sinners?'" (Luke 5:30 NCV).

Enter the religious police and their thin-lipped piety. Big black books under arms. Cheerful as Siberian prison guards. Clerical collars so tight that veins bulge. They like to grill too. But not steaks.

Matthew is the first to feel the heat. "Some religious fellow you are," one says, practically pulling an eyebrow muscle. "Look at the people you hang out with."

Matthew doesn't know whether to get mad or get out. Before he has time to choose, Jesus intervenes, explaining that Matthew is right where he needs to be. "Healthy people don't need a doctor—sick people do. I have come to call sinners to turn from their sins, not to spend my time with those who think they are already good enough" (vv. 31–32 NLT).

Quite a story. Matthew goes from double-dealer to disciple. He throws a party that makes the religious right uptight, but Christ proud. The good guys look good, and the bad guys hit the road. Some story indeed.

What do we do with it?

That depends on which side of the tax collector's table you find yourself. You and I are Matthew. Don't look at me that way. There's enough hustler in the best of us to qualify for Matthew's table. Maybe you've never taken taxes, but you've taken liberty with the truth, taken credit that wasn't yours, taken advantage of the weak. You and me? Matthew.

If you're still at the table, you receive an invitation. "Follow me." So what if you've got a rube reputation? So did Matthew. You may end up writing your own gospel.

If you've left the table, you receive a clarification. You don't have to be weird to follow Jesus. You don't have to stop liking your friends to follow him. Just the opposite. A few introductions would be nice. Do you know how to grill a steak?

Sometime ago I was asked to play a game of golf. The foursome included two preachers, a church leader, and a "Matthew, B.C." The thought of four hours with three Christians, two of whom were pulpiteers, did not appeal to him. His best friend, a Christ follower and his boss, insisted, so he agreed. I'm happy to report that he proclaimed the experience painless. On the ninth hole he turned to one of us and said, smiling, "I'm so glad you guys are normal." I think he meant this: "I'm glad you didn't get in my face or club me with a King James driver. Thanks for laughing at my jokes and telling a few yourself. Thanks for being normal." We didn't lower standards. But neither did we saddle a high horse. We were nice. Normal and nice.

Discipleship is sometimes defined by being normal.

A woman in a small Arkansas community was a single mom with a frail baby. Her neighbor would stop by every few days and keep the child so she could shop. After some weeks her neighbor shared more than time; she shared her faith, and the woman did what Matthew did. She followed Christ.

The friends of the young mother objected. "Do you know what those people teach?" they contested.

"Here is what I know," she told them. "They held my baby."[1]

I think Jesus likes that kind of answer, don't you?

4

The Hand God Loves to Hold

Desperate People

MARK 5:25–34

To see her hand you need to look low. Look down. That's where she lives. Low to the ground. Low on the priority list. Low on the social scale. She's low.

Can you see it? Her hand? Gnarled. Thin. Diseased. Dirt blackens the nails and stains the skin. Look carefully amid the knees and feet of the crowd. They're scampering after Christ. He walks. She crawls. People bump her, but she doesn't stop. Others complain. She doesn't care. The woman is desperate. Blood won't stay in her body. "There was a woman in the crowd who had had a hemorrhage for twelve years" (Mark 5:25 NLT). Twelve years of clinics. Treatments. Herbs. Prayer meetings. Incantations.

"She had suffered a great deal from many doctors through the years" (v. 26 NLT). Do you smell quackery in those words? Doctors who took, not the disease, but advantage of her? She "had spent everything she had to pay them, but she had gotten no better. In fact, she was worse" (v. 26 NLT).

No health. No money. And no family to help. Unclean, according to the Law of Moses. The Law protected women from aggressive, insensitive men during those times of the month. In this woman's case severe application of the Law left her, not untouched, but untouchable, ceremonially unclean. The hand you see in the crowd? The one reaching for the robe? No one will touch it.

Wasn't always the case. Surely a husband once took it in marriage. The hand looked different in those days: clean, soft skinned, perfumed. A husband once loved this hand.

A family once relied on this hand. To cook, sew. To wipe tears from cheeks, tuck blankets under chins. Are the hands of a mother ever still?

Only if she is diseased.

Maybe the husband tried to stay with her, carting her to doctors and treatment centers. Or maybe he gave up quickly, overwhelmed by her naps, nausea, and anemia. So he put her out. A change of clothes and a handful of change—that's it. Close the door.

So she has nothing. No money. No home. No health. Dilapidated dreams. Deflated faith. Unwelcome in the synagogue. Unwanted by her community. For twelve years she has suffered. She has nothing, and her health is getting worse.

Maybe that's what did it. She "had grown worse" (v. 26). This morning she could scarcely stand. She splashed water on her face and was horrified by the skeletal image in the pool. What you and I see in Auschwitz photos, she saw in her reflection—gaunt cheeks, tired and taut skin, and two full-moon eyes.

She is desperate. And her desperation births an idea.

"She had heard about Jesus" (v. 27 NLT). Every society has a grapevine, even—or especially—the society of the sick. Word among the lepers and the left out is this: Jesus can heal. And Jesus is coming. By invitation of the synagogue ruler, Jesus is coming to Capernaum.

Odd to find the ruler and the woman in the same story. He powerful. She pitiful. He in demand. She insignificant. He is high. She is low. But his daughter is dying. Tragedy levels social topography. So they find themselves on the same path in the village and the same page of the Bible.

As the crowd comes, she thinks, "If I can just touch his clothing, I will be healed" (v. 28 NLT). At the right time, she crab-scurries through the crowd. Knees bump her ribs. "Move out of the way!" someone shouts. She doesn't care and doesn't stop. Twelve years on the streets have toughened her.

Jesus' robe is in sight. Four tassels dangle from blue threads. Ornaments of holiness worn by Jewish men. How long since she has touched anything holy? She extends her hand toward a tassel.

Her sick hand. Her tired hand. The hand the husband no longer wants and the family no longer needs. She touches the robe of Jesus, and "immediately the bleeding stopped, and she could feel that she had been healed!" (v. 29 NLT).

Life rushes in. Pale cheeks turn pink. Shallow breaths become full. Hoover Dam cracks and a river floods. The woman feels power enter. And

Jesus? Jesus feels power exit. "Jesus realized at once that healing power had gone out from him, so he turned around in the crowd and asked, 'Who touched my clothes?'" (v. 30 NLT).

Did Christ surprise even Christ? Has Jesus the divine moved faster than Jesus the human? The Savior outstepped the neighbor? "Who touched my clothes?"

His disciples think the query is odd. "'All this crowd is pressing around you. How can you ask, "Who touched me?"' But he kept on looking around to see who had done it" (vv. 31–32 NLT).

Can we fault this woman's timidity? She doesn't know what to expect. Jesus could berate her, embarrass her. Besides, he was her last choice. She sought the help of a dozen others before she sought his. And the people— what will they do? What will the ruler of the synagogue do? He is upright. She is unclean. And here she is, lunging at the town guest. No wonder she is afraid.

But she has one reason to have courage. She is healed. "The woman, knowing what had happened, knowing she was the one, stepped up in fear and trembling, knelt before him, and gave him the whole story" (v. 33 MSG).

"The whole story." How long had it been since someone put the gear of life in Park, turned off the key, and listened to her story? But when this woman reaches out to Jesus, he does. With the town bishop waiting, a young girl dying, and a crowd pressing, he still makes time for a woman from the fringe. Using a term he gives to no one else, he says, "Daughter, your faith has made you well. Go in peace. You have been healed" (v. 34 NLT).

And Christ moves on.

And she moves on.

But we can't. We can't because we've been there. Been her. Are there. Are her. Desperate. Dirty. Drained.

Illness took her strength. What took yours? Red ink? Hard drink? Late nights in the wrong arms? Long days on the wrong job? Pregnant too soon? Too often? Is her hand your hand? If so, take heart. Your family may shun it. Society may avoid it. But Christ? Christ wants to touch it. When your hand reaches through the masses, he knows.

Yours is the hand he loves to hold.

5

Try Again

Discouraged People

LUKE 5:1–11

There is a look that says, "It's too late." You've seen it. The rolling of the eyes, the shaking of the head, the pursing of the lips.

Your friend is a day from divorce. Over coffee you urge, "Can't you try one more time?"

She shrugs. "Done that."

Your father and brother don't speak to one another. Haven't for years. "Won't you try again?" you ask your dad. He looks away, inhales deeply, and sighs.

Five years this side of retirement the economy Hindenburgs your husband's retirement. You try to make the best of it. "You can go back to school. Learn a new trade." You might as well have told him to swim to London. He shakes his head. "I'm too old . . . It's too late."

Too late to save a marriage.

Too late to reconcile.

Too late for a new career.

Too late to catch any fish. Or so Peter thinks. All night he fished. He witnessed both the setting and the rising of the sun but has nothing to show for it. While other fishermen cleaned their catch, he just cleaned his nets. But now Jesus wants him to try again.

"Now it happened that while the crowd was pressing around Him and listening to the word of God, [Jesus] was standing by the lake of Gennesaret" (Luke 5:1).

The Sea of Gennesaret, or Galilee, is a six-by-thirteen-mile body of water in northern Israel. These days her shore sleeps, attracting only a cluster of tour buses and a handful of fishermen. But in the days of Jesus the area bustled with people. Nine of the seacoast villages boasted populations of fifteen thousand plus. And you get the impression that a good portion of those people was present the morning Christ ministered on the beach. As more people arrived, more people pressed. With every press, Jesus took a step back. Soon he was stepping off the sand and into the water. That's when he had an idea.

> He saw two boats lying at the edge of the lake; but the fishermen had gotten out of them and were washing their nets. And He got into one of the boats, which was Simon's, and asked him to put out a little way from the land. And He sat down and began teaching the people from the boat. When He had finished speaking, He said to Simon, "Put out into the deep water and let down your nets for a catch." (vv. 2–4)

Jesus needs a boat; Peter provides one. Jesus preaches; Peter is content to listen. Jesus suggests a midmorning fishing trip, however, and Peter gives him a look. The it's-too-late look. He runs his fingers through his hair and sighs, "Master, we worked hard all night and caught nothing" (v. 5). Can you feel Peter's futility?

All night the boat floated fishless on the black sheet of the sea. Lanterns of distant vessels bounced like fireflies. The men swung their nets and filled the air with the percussion of their trade.

Swish, slap . . . silence.

Swish, slap . . . silence.

Midnight.

Excited voices from across the lake reached the men. Another boat had found a school. Peter considered moving but decided against it.

Swish, slap . . . silence.

Two o'clock in the morning. Peter rested while his brother fished. Then Andrew rested. James, floating nearby, suggested a move. The others agreed. Wind billowed the sails and blew the boats to a cove. The rhythm resumed.

Swish, slap . . . silence.

Every yank of the net was easy. Too easy. This night the lake was a proper lady. No matter how often the men winked and whistled, she offered nothing.

Golden shafts eventually reclaimed the sky. Most mornings the sunrise inspires the men. Today it only tired them. They didn't want to see it. Who wants to dock an empty boat? Who wants to tie up and clean up, knowing the first question the wife is going to ask? And, most of all, who wants to hear a well-rested carpenter-turned-rabbi say, "Put out into the deep water and let down your nets for a catch" (v. 4)?

Oh, the thoughts Peter might have had. *I'm tired. Bone tired. I want a meal and a bed, not a fishing trip. Am I his tour guide? Besides, half of Galilee is watching. I feel like a loser already. Now he wants to put on a midmorning fishing exhibition? You can't catch fish in the morning. Count me out.*

Whatever thoughts Peter had were distilled to one phrase: "We worked hard all night and caught nothing" (v. 5).

Do you have any worn, wet, empty nets? Do you know the feeling of a sleepless, fishless night? Of course you do. For what have you been casting?

Sobriety? "I've worked so hard to stay sober, but . . ."

Solvency? "My debt is an anvil around my neck . . ."

Faith? "I want to believe, but . . ."

Healing? "I've been sick so long . . ."

A happy marriage? "No matter what I do . . ."

I've worked hard all night and caught nothing.

You've felt what Peter felt. You've sat where Peter sat. And now Jesus is asking you to go fishing. He knows your nets are empty. He knows your heart is weary. He knows you'd like nothing more than to turn your back on the mess and call it a life.

But he urges, "It's not too late to try again."

See if Peter's reply won't help you formulate your own. "I will do as You say and let down the nets" (v. 5).

Not much passion in those words. You might hope for a ten-thousand-candle smile and a fist pumping the air. "I got Jesus in my boat. Momma, warm up the oven!" But Peter shows no excitement. He feels none. Now he has to unfold the nets, pull out the oars, and convince James and John to postpone their rest. He has to work. If faith is measured in seeds, his is an angstrom. Inspired? No. But obedient? Admirably. And an angstrom of obedience is all Jesus wants.

"Put out into the deep water," the God-man instructs.

Why the deep water? You suppose Jesus knew something Peter didn't?

You suppose Jesus is doing with Peter what we parents do with our kids on Easter Sunday? They find most of the eggs on their own. But a couple of treasures inevitably survive the first harvest. "Look," I'd whisper in the ears of my daughters, "behind the tree." A quick search around the trunk, and, what do you know, Dad was right. Spotting treasures is easy for the one who hid them. Finding fish is simple for the God who made them. To Jesus, the Sea of Galilee is a dollar-store fishbowl on a kitchen cabinet.

Peter gives the net a swish, lets it slap, and watches it disappear. Luke doesn't tell us what Peter did while he was waiting for the net to sink, so I will. (I'm glancing heavenward for lightning.)

I like to think that Peter, while holding the net, looks over his shoulder at Jesus. And I like to think that Jesus, knowing Peter is about to be half yanked into the water, starts to smile. A daddy-daughter-Easter-egg smile. Rising cheeks render his eyes half-moons. A dash of white flashes beneath his whiskers. Jesus tries to hold it back but can't.

There is so much to smile about. It's Easter Sunday, and the lawn is crawling with kids. Just wait till they look under the tree.

> When they had done this, they enclosed a great quantity of fish, and their nets began to break; so they signaled to their partners in the other boat for them to come and help them. And they came and filled both of the boats, so that they began to sink. (vv. 6–7)

Peter's arm is yanked into the water. It's all he can do to hang on until the other guys can help. Within moments the four fishermen and the carpenter are up to their knees in flopping silver.

Peter lifts his eyes off the catch and onto the face of Christ. In that moment, for the first time, he sees Jesus. Not Jesus the Fish Finder. Not Jesus the Multitude Magnet. Not Jesus the Rabbi. Peter sees Jesus the Lord.

Peter falls face first among the fish. Their stink doesn't bother him. It is his stink that he's worried about. "Go away from me Lord, for I am a sinful man!" (v. 8).

Christ had no intention of honoring that request. He doesn't abandon self-confessed schlemiels. Quite the contrary, he enlists them. "Do not fear, from now on you will be catching men" (v. 10).

Contrary to what you may have been told, Jesus doesn't limit his recruiting to the stout-hearted. The beat up and worn out are prime prospects in his book, and he's been known to climb into boats, bars, and brothels to tell them, "It's not too late to start over."

Peter learned the lesson. But wouldn't you know it? Peter forgot the lesson. Two short years later this man who confessed Christ in the boat cursed Christ at a fire. The night before Jesus' crucifixion, Peter told people that he'd never heard of Jesus.

He couldn't have made a more tragic mistake. He knew it. The burly fisherman buried his bearded face in thick hands and spent Friday night in tears. All the feelings of that Galilean morning came back to him.

It's too late.

But then Sunday came. Jesus came! Peter saw him. Peter was convinced that Christ had come back from the dead. But apparently Peter wasn't convinced that Christ came back for him.

So he went back to the boat—to the same boat, the same beach, the same sea. He came out of retirement. He and his buddies washed the barnacles off the hull, unpacked the nets, and pushed out. They fished all night, and, honest to Pete, they caught nothing.

Poor Peter. Blew it as a disciple. Now he's blowing it as a fisherman. About the time he wonders if it's too late to take up carpentry, the sky turns orange, and they hear a voice from the coastline. "Had any luck?"

They yell back, "No."

"Try the right side of the boat!"

With nothing to lose and no more pride to protect, they give it a go. "So they cast, and then they were not able to haul it in because of the great number of fish" (John 21:6). It takes a moment for the déjà vu to hit Peter. But when it does, he cannonballs into the water and swims as fast as he can to see the one who loved him enough to *re-create* a miracle. This time the message stuck.

Peter never again fished for fish. He spent the rest of his days telling anyone who would listen, "It's not too late to try again."

Is it too late for you? Before you say yes, before you fold up the nets and head for the house—two questions. Have you given Christ your boat? Your heartache? Your dead-end dilemma? Your struggle? Have you really turned it over to him? And have you gone deep? Have you bypassed the surface-water solutions you can see in search of the deep-channel provisions God can give? Try the other side of the boat. Go deeper than you've gone. You may find what Peter found. The payload of his second effort was not the fish he caught but the God he saw.

The God-man who spots weary fishermen, who cares enough to enter their boats, who will turn his back on the adoration of a crowd to solve the frustration of a friend. The next door Savior who whispers this word to the owners of empty nets, "Let's try again—this time with me on board."

6

Spit Therapy

Suffering People

JOHN 9:1–38

The old guy at the corner hasn't seen him. The woman selling the figs hasn't either. Jesus describes him to the scribes at the gate and the kids in the courtyard. "He's about this tall. Clothes are ragged. Belly-length beard."

No one has a clue.

For the better part of a day Jesus has been searching up and down the Jerusalem streets. He didn't stop for lunch. Hasn't paused to rest. The only time his feet aren't moving is when he is asking, "Pardon me, but have you seen the fellow who used to beg on the corner?"

He searched the horse stable and checked out the roof of a shed. Now Jesus is going door-to-door. "He has a homeless look," Jesus tells people. "Unkempt. Dirty. And he has muddy eyelids."

Finally a boy gives him a lead. Jesus takes a back street toward the temple and spots the man sitting on a stump between two donkeys. Christ approaches from behind and places a hand on his shoulder. "There you are! I've been looking for you." The fellow turns and, for the first time, sees the one who let him see. And what the man does next you may find hard to believe.

Let me catch you up. John introduces him to us with these words. "As [Jesus] passed by, He saw a man blind from birth" (John 9:1). This man has never seen a sunrise. Can't tell purple from pink. The disciples fault the family tree. "Rabbi, who sinned, this man or his parents, that he would be born blind?" (v. 2).

Neither, the God-man replies. Trace this condition back to heaven. The reason the man was born sightless? So "the works of God might be displayed in him" (v. 3).

Talk about a thankless role. Selected to suffer. Some sing to God's glory.

43

Others teach to God's glory. Who wants to be blind for God's glory? Which is tougher—the condition or discovering it was God's idea?

The cure proves to be as surprising as the cause. "[Jesus] spat on the ground, and made clay of the spittle, and applied the clay to his eyes" (v. 6).

The world abounds with paintings of the God-man: in the arms of Mary, in the Garden of Gethsemane, in the Upper Room, in the darkened tomb. Jesus touching. Jesus weeping, laughing, teaching . . . but I've never seen a painting of Jesus spitting.

Christ smacking his lips a time or two, gathering a mouth of saliva, working up a blob of drool, and letting it go. Down in the dirt. (Kids, next time your mother tells you not to spit, show her this passage.) Then he squats, stirs up a puddle of . . . I don't know, what would you call it?

Holy putty? Spit therapy? Saliva solution? Whatever the name, he places a fingerful in his palm, and then, as calmly as a painter spackles a hole in the wall, Jesus streaks mud-miracle on the blind man's eyes. "Go, wash in the pool of Siloam" (v. 7).

The beggar feels his way to the pool, splashes water on his mud-streaked face, and rubs away the clay. The result is the first chapter of Genesis, just for him. Light where there was darkness. Virgin eyes focus, fuzzy figures become human beings, and John receives the Understatement of the Bible Award when he writes: "He . . . came back seeing" (v. 7).

Come on, John! Running short of verbs? How about "he *raced* back seeing"? "He *danced* back seeing"? "He *roared* back whooping and hollering and kissing everything he could, for the first time, see"? The guy had to be thrilled.

We would love to leave him that way, but if this man's life were a cafeteria line, he would have just stepped from the sirloin to the boiled Brussels sprouts. Look at the reaction of the neighbors: "'Is not this the one who used to sit and beg?' Others were saying, 'This is he,' still others were saying, 'No, but he is like him.' He kept saying, 'I am the one'" (vv. 8–9).

These folks don't celebrate; they debate! They have watched this man grope and trip since he was a kid (v. 20). You'd think they would rejoice. But they don't. They march him down to the church to have him kosher tested. When the Pharisees ask for an explanation, the was-blind beggar says, "He applied clay to my eyes, and I washed, and I see" (v. 15).

Again we pause for the applause, but none comes. No recognition. No celebration. Apparently Jesus failed to consult the healing handbook. "Now it was a Sabbath on the day when Jesus made the clay and opened his eyes. . . . The Pharisees were saying, 'This man is not from God, because He does not keep the Sabbath'" (vv. 14, 16).

That noise you hear is the beeping of the absurdity Geiger counter. The religious leaders' verdict bounces the needle. Here is a parallel response. Suppose the swimming pool where you recreate has a sign on the fence that reads Rescues Performed by Certified Lifeguards Only. You never think good or bad about the rule until one day you bang your head on the bottom. You black out, ten feet under.

Next thing you know you're belly down on the side of the pool, coughing up water. Someone rescued you. And when the lifeguards appear, the fellow who pulled you out of the deep disappears. As you come to your senses, you tell the story. But rather than rejoice, people recoil. "Doesn't count! Doesn't count!" they shout like referees waving off a basketball that cleared the net after the clock had expired. "It wasn't official. Wasn't legal. Since the rescuer wasn't certified, consider yourself drowned."

Duh? You bet. Will no one rejoice with this man? The neighbors didn't. The preachers didn't. Wait, here come the parents. But the reaction of the formerly blind man's parents is even worse.

> They called the parents of the very one who had received his sight, and questioned them, saying, "Is this your son, who you say was born blind? Then how does he now see?" His parents answered them and said, "We know that this is our son, and that he was born blind; but how he now sees, we do not know; or who opened his eyes, we do not know. Ask him; he is of age, he will speak for himself." His parents said this because they were afraid of the Jews; for the Jews had already agreed that if anyone confessed Him to be Christ, he was to be put out of the synagogue. (vv. 18–22)

How can they do this? Granted, to be put out of the synagogue is serious. But isn't refusing to help your child even more so?

Who was really blind that day? The neighbors didn't see the man; they saw a novelty. The church leaders didn't see the man; they saw a technicality. The parents didn't see their son; they saw a social difficulty. In the end, no one saw him. "So they put him out" (v. 34).

And now, here he is, on a back street of Jerusalem. The fellow has to be bewildered. Born blind only to be healed. Healed only to be kicked out. Kicked out only to be left alone. The peak of Everest and the heat of Sahara, all in one Sabbath. Now he can't even beg anymore. How would that feel?

You may know all too well. I know of a man who has buried four children. A single mother in our church is raising two autistic sons. We buried a neighbor whose cancer led to heart trouble, which created pneumonia. Her health record was as thick as a phone book. Do some people seem to be dealt more than their share of bad hands?

If so, Jesus knows. He knows how they feel, and he knows where they are. "Jesus heard that they had thrown him out, and went and found him" (v. 35 MSG). In case the stable birth wasn't enough. If three decades of earth walking and miracle working are insufficient. If there be any doubt regarding God's full-bore devotion, he does things like this. He tracks down a troubled pauper.

The beggar lifts his eyes to look into the face of the One who started all this. Is he going to criticize Christ? Complain to Christ? You couldn't blame him for doing both. After all, he didn't volunteer for the disease or the deliverance. But he does neither. No, "he worshiped Him" (v. 38). Don't you know he knelt? Don't you think he wept? And how could he keep from wrapping his arms around the waist of the One who gave him sight? He worshiped him.

And when you see him, you will too.

How dare I make such a statement? This book will be held by arthritic hands. These chapters will be read by tear-filled eyes. Some of your legs are wheelchaired, and your hearts are hope starved. But "these hard times are small potatoes compared to the coming good times, the lavish celebration prepared for us" (2 Cor. 4:17 MSG).

The day you see your Savior you will experience a million times over what Joni Eareckson Tada experienced on her wedding day. Are you acquainted with her story? A diving accident left her paralyzed at the age of seventeen. Nearly all of her fifty-plus years have been spent in a wheelchair. Her handicap doesn't keep her from writing or painting or speaking about her Savior. Nor did her handicap keep her from marrying Ken. But it almost kept her from the joy of the wedding.

She'd done her best. Her gown was draped over a thin wire mesh covering the wheels of her wheelchair. With flowers in her lap and a sparkle in her eye, she felt a "little like a float in the Rose Parade."

A ramp had been constructed, connecting the foyer to the altar. While waiting her turn to motorize over it, Joni made a discovery. Across her dress was a big, black grease mark courtesy of the chair. And the chair, though "spiffed up . . . was still the big, clunky thing it always was." Then the bouquet of daisies on her lap slid off center; her paralyzed hands were unable to rearrange them. She felt far from the picture-perfect bride of *Bride's Magazine.*

She inched her chair forward and looked down the aisle. That's when she saw her groom.

I spotted him way down front, standing at attention and looking tall and elegant in his formal attire. My face grew hot. My heart began to pound. Our eyes met and, amazingly, from that point everything changed.

How I looked no longer mattered. I forgot all about my wheelchair. Grease stains? Flowers out of place? Who cares? No longer did I feel ugly or unworthy; the love in Ken's eyes washed it all away. I was the pure and perfect bride. That's what he saw, and that's what changed me. It took great restraint not to jam my "power stick" into high gear and race down the aisle to be with my groom.[1]

When she saw him, she forgot about herself.

When you see him, you will too.

I'm sorry about your greasy gown. And your flowers—they tend to slide, don't they? Who has an answer for the diseases, drudgeries, and darkness of this life? I don't. But we do know this. Everything changes when you look at your groom.

And yours is coming. Just as he came for the blind man, Jesus is coming for you. The hand that touched the blind man's shoulder will touch your cheeks. The face that changed his life will change yours.

And when you see Jesus, you will bow in worship.

7

What Jesus Says at Funerals

Grieving People

JOHN 11:1–44

Y ou never know what to say at funerals. This one is no exception. The chapel is library quiet. People acknowledge each other with soft smiles and nods. You say nothing.

What's to be said? There's a dead body in the place, for crying out loud! Just last month you took the guy out to lunch. You and Lazarus told jokes over nachos. Aside from a bad cough, you thought he was healthy.

Within a week you learned of the diagnosis. The doctor gave him sixty days. He didn't make it that long. Now you're both at his funeral. He in the casket. You in the pew. Death has silenced you both.

The church is full, so you stand at the back. Stained glass prisms the afternoon sun, streaking faces with shafts of purple and gold. You recognize many of them. Bethany is a small town. The two women on the front pew you know well. Martha and Mary are the sisters of Lazarus. Quiet, pensive Mary. Bustling, busy Martha. Even now she can't sit still. She keeps looking over her shoulder. *Who for?* you wonder.

In a matter of moments the answer enters. And when he does, she rushes up the aisle to meet him. Had you not known his name, the many whispers would have informed you. "It's Jesus." Every head turns.

He's wearing a tie, though you get the impression he rarely does. His collar seems tight and his jacket dated. A dozen or so men follow him; some stand in the aisle, others in the foyer. They have a well-traveled, wrinkled look, as if they rode all night.

Jesus embraces Martha, and she weeps. As she weeps, you wonder. You wonder what Jesus is going to do. You wonder what Jesus is going to say. He spoke to the winds and the demons. Remarkable. But death? Does he have anything to say about death? Your thoughts are interrupted by

Martha's accusation: "Lord, if You had been here, my brother would not have died" (John 11:21).

You can't fault her frustration. Are she and Jesus not friends? When Jesus and his followers had nowhere else to go, "Martha welcomed them into her home" (Luke 10:38 TLB). Mary and Martha know Jesus. They know Jesus loves Lazarus. "Lord," they told the courier to tell him, "the one you love is very sick" (John 11:3 NLT). This is no fan-mail request. This is a friend needing help.

Desperately needing help. The Greek language has two principle words to express sickness: one describes the presence of a disease, the other its effects. Martha uses the latter. A fair translation of her appeal would be, "Lord, the one you love is sinking fast."

Friends send Christ an urgent appeal in a humble fashion, and what does he do? "He stayed where he was for the next two days and did not go to them" (v. 6 NLT). By the time he arrives, Martha is so broken up she hardly knows what to say. With one breath she rebukes: "Lord, if You had been here, my brother would not have died" (v. 21). With the next she resolves: "But even now I know that whatever You ask of God, God will give You" (v. 22 NKJV).

Every funeral has its Marthas. Sprinkled among the bereaved are the bewildered. "Help me understand this one, Jesus."

This has been the prayer of Karen Burris Davis ever since that November morning when her son—and, consequently, her sun—failed to rise. Jacob was thirteen. The picture of health. Four medical examiners have found no cause of death. Her answer, she says, is no answer.

> I miss Jacob so much that I am not sure I can do this. I stand at the cemetery, knowing his body is down there, and think how insane it is to feel like if I start digging, I could see him just one more time. I just so much want to smell his hair and touch him. . . . How quickly the scent of someone goes away. I would have thought it would have lingered forever, that sour boy smell and those stinky tennis shoes. Of course, sometimes he actually did smell of soap and shampoo. The house is so empty without all his noise and plans.[1]

Grief fogs in the heart like a Maine-coast morning. The mourner hears the waves but sees no water. Detects voices but no faces. The life of the brokenhearted becomes that of a "footwatcher, walking through airports or the grocery store staring at feet, methodically moving through a misty world. One foot, then the other."[2]

Martha sat in a damp world, cloudy, tearful. And Jesus sat in it with her. "I am the resurrection and the life. Those who believe in me, even though they die like everyone else, will live again" (v. 25 NLT). Hear those words in a Superman tone, if you like. Clark Kent descending from nowhere, ripping shirt and popping buttons to reveal the *S* beneath. "I AM THE RESURRECTION AND THE LIFE!!!" Do you see a Savior with Terminator tenderness bypassing the tears of Martha and Mary and, in doing so, telling them and all grievers to buck up and trust?

I don't. I don't because of what Jesus does next. He weeps. He sits on the pew between Mary and Martha, puts an arm around each, and sobs. Among the three, a tsunami of sorrow is stirred; a monsoon of tears is released. Tears that reduce to streaks the watercolor conceptions of a cavalier Christ. Jesus weeps.

He weeps with them.

He weeps for them.

He weeps with you.

He weeps for you.

He weeps so we will know: Mourning is not disbelieving. Flooded eyes don't represent a faithless heart. A person can enter a cemetery Jesus-certain of life after death and still have a Twin Tower crater in the heart. Christ did. He wept, and he knew he was ten minutes from seeing a living Lazarus!

And his tears give you permission to shed your own. Grief does not mean you don't trust; it simply means you can't stand the thought of another day without the Jacob or Lazarus of your life. If Jesus gave the love, he understands the tears. So grieve, but don't grieve like those who don't know the rest of this story.

Jesus touches Martha's cheek, gives Mary a hug, stands, and turns to face the corpse. The casket lid is closed. He tells Martha to have it opened. She shakes her head and starts to refuse but then pauses. Turning to the funeral home director, she says, "Open it."

Since you are standing, you can see the face of Lazarus. It's waxy and white. You think Jesus is going to weep again. You never expect him to speak to his friend.

But he does. A few feet from the casket Jesus yells, "Lazarus, come out!" (v. 43 NCV).

Preachers always address the living. But the dead? One thing is sure. There better be a rumble in that casket, or this preacher is going to therapy. You and everyone else hear the rumble. There is movement in the coffin. "He who had died came out" (v. 44 NKJV).

Dead men don't do that—do they? Dead men don't come out. Dead men don't wake up. Dead hearts don't beat. Dried blood doesn't rush. Empty lungs don't inhale. No, dead men don't come out—unless they hear the voice of the Lord of life.

The ears of the dead may be deaf to your voice and mine but not to his. Christ is "Lord of both the dead and the living" (Rom. 14:9 NIV). When Christ speaks to the dead, the dead listen. Indeed, had Jesus not addressed Lazarus by name, the tenant of every tomb on earth would have stepped forth.

Lazarus jolts up in the coffin, blinks, and looks around the room as if someone carted him there during a nap. A woman screams. Another faints. Everyone shouts. And you? You learned something. You learned what to say at funerals.

You learned there is a time to say nothing. Your words can't dispel a fog, but your presence can warm it. And your words can't give a Lazarus back to his sisters. But God's can. And it's just a matter of time before he speaks. "The Lord himself will come down from heaven with a commanding shout. . . . All the Christians who have died will rise from their graves" (1 Thess. 4:16 NLT).

Till then, we grieve, but not like those who have no hope.

And we listen. We listen for his voice. For we know who has the final say about death.

8

Getting the Hell Out

Tormented People

MARK 5:2-20

> When He got out of the boat, immediately a man from the tombs with an unclean spirit met Him, and he had his dwelling among the tombs. And no one was able to bind him anymore, even with a chain; because he had often been bound with shackles and chains, and the chains had been torn apart by him and the shackles broken in pieces, and no one was strong enough to subdue him. Constantly, night and day, he was screaming among the tombs and in the mountains, and gashing himself with stones. (Mark 5:2-5)

Wiry, clumpy hair. A beard to the chest, ribboned with blood. Furtive eyes, darting in all directions, refusing to fix. Naked. No sandals to protect feet from the rocks of the ground or clothing to protect skin from the rocks of his hand. He beats himself with stones. Bruises blotch his skin like ink stains. Open sores and gashes attract flies.

His home is a limestone mausoleum, a graveyard of Galilean shoreline caves cut out of the cliffs. Apparently he feels more secure among the dead than the living.

Which pleases the living. He baffles them. See the cracked shackles on his legs and broken chains on his wrists? They can't control the guy. Nothing holds him. How do you manage chaos? Travelers skirt the area out of fear (Matt. 8:28). The villagers were left with a problem, and we are left with a picture—a picture of the work of Satan.

How else do we explain our bizarre behavior? The violent rages of a father. The secret binges of a mother. The sudden rebellion of a teenager. Maxed-out credit cards, Internet pornography. Satan does not sit still. A glimpse of the wild man reveals Satan's goal for you and me.

Self-imposed pain. The demoniac used rocks. We are more sophisticated; we use drugs, sex, work, violence, and food. (Hell makes us hurt ourselves.)

Obsession with death and darkness. Even unchained, the wild man loitered among the dead. Evil feels at home there. Communing with the deceased, sacrificing the living, a morbid fascination with death and dying—this is not the work of God.

Endless restlessness. The man on the eastern shore screamed day and night (Mark 5:5). Satan begets raging frenzy. "The evil spirit . . . wanders . . . ," Jesus says, "looking for rest" (Matt. 12:43 PHILLIPS).

Isolation. The man is all alone in his suffering. Such is Satan's plan. "The devil prowls around like a roaring lion, seeking some *one* to devour" (1 Pet. 5:8 RSV, emphasis mine). Fellowship foils his work.

And Jesus?

Jesus wrecks his work. Christ steps out of the boat with both pistols blasting. "Come out of the man, unclean spirit!" (Mark 5:8 NKJV).

No chitchat. No niceties. No salutations. Demons deserve no tolerance. They throw themselves at the feet and mercy of Christ. The leader of the horde begs for the others:

> "What have you to do with me, Jesus, Son of the Most High God? I adjure you by God, do not torment me." . . . Jesus asked him, "What is your name?" He replied, "My name is Legion; for we are many." He begged him earnestly not to send them out of the country. (vv. 7, 9–10 NRSV)

Legion is a Roman military term. A Roman legion involved six thousand soldiers. To envision that many demons inhabiting this man is frightening but not unrealistic. What bats are to a cave, demons are to hell—too many to number.

The demons are not only numerous, they are equipped. A legion is a battalion in arms. Satan and his friends come to fight. Hence, we are urged to "take up the full armor of God, so that you will be able to resist in the evil day, and having done everything, to stand firm" (Eph. 6:13).

Well we should, for they are organized. "We are fighting against forces and authorities and against rulers of darkness and powers in the spiritual world" (Eph. 6:12 CEV). Jesus spoke of the "gates of hell" (Matt. 16:18 KJV), a phrase that suggests the "council of hell." Our enemy has a complex and conniving spiritual army. Dismiss any image of a red-suited Satan with pitchfork and pointy tail. The devil is a strong devil.

But, and this is the point of the passage, in God's presence, the devil is a wimp. Satan is to God what a mosquito is to an atomic bomb.

> Now a large herd of swine was feeding there near the mountains. So all the demons begged Him, saying, "Send us to the swine, that we may enter them." And at once Jesus gave them permission. Then the unclean spirits went out and entered the swine (there were about two thousand); and the herd ran violently down the steep place into the sea, and drowned in the sea. (Mark 5:11–13 NKJV)

How hell's court cowers in Christ's presence! Demons bow before him, solicit him, and obey him. They can't even lease a pig without his permission. Then how do we explain Satan's influence?

Natalie[1] must have asked that question a thousand times. In the list of characters for a modern-day Gerasenes story, her name is near the top. She was raised in a tormented world.

The community suspected nothing. Her parents cast a friendly façade. Each Sunday they paraded Natalie and her sisters down the church aisle. Her father served as an elder. Her mom played the organ. The congregation respected them. Natalie despised them. To this day she refuses to call her parents "Mom" and "Dad." A "warlock" and "witch" don't deserve the distinction.

When she was six months old, they sexually sacrificed Natalie on hell's altar, tagging her as a sex object to be exploited by men in any place, anytime. Cultists bipolarized her world: dressing her in white for Sunday service and, hours later, stripping her at the coven. If she didn't scream or vomit during the attack, Natalie was rewarded with an ice-cream cone. Only by "crawling down deep" inside herself could she survive.

Natalie miraculously escaped the cult but not the memories. Well into her adult years, she wore six pairs of underpants as a wall of protection. Dresses created vulnerability; she avoided them. She hated being a woman; she hated seeing men; she hated being alive. Only God could know the legion of terrors that dogged her. But God did know.

Hidden within the swampland of her soul was an untouched island.

Small but safe. Built, she believes, by her heavenly Father during the hours the little girl sat on a church pew. Words of his love, hymns of his mercy—they left their mark. She learned to retreat to this island and pray. God heard her prayers. Counselors came. Hope began to offset horror. Her faith increasingly outweighed her fears. The healing process was lengthy and tedious but victorious, culminating in her marriage to a godly man.[2]

Her deliverance didn't include cliffs and pigs, but, make no mistake, she was delivered. And we are reminded. Satan can disturb us, but he cannot defeat us. The head of the serpent is crushed.

I saw a literal picture of this in a prairie ditch. A petroleum company was hiring strong backs and weak minds to lay a pipeline. Since I qualified, much of a high-school summer was spent shoveling in a shoulder-high, multimile West Texas trough. A large digging machine trenched ahead of us. We followed, scooping out the excess dirt and rocks.

One afternoon the machine dislodged more than dirt. "Snake!" shouted the foreman. We popped out of that hole faster than a jack-in-the-box and looked down at the rattlesnake nest. Big momma hissed, and her little kids squirmed. Reentering the trench was not an option. One worker launched his shovel and beheaded the rattler. We stood on the higher ground and watched as she—now headless—writhed and twisted in the soft dirt below. Though defanged, the snake still spooked us.

Gee, Max, thanks for the inspirational image.

Inspirational? Maybe not. But hopeful? I think so. That scene in the West Texas summer is a parable of where we are in life. Is the devil not a snake? John calls him "that old snake who is the devil" (Rev. 20:2 NCV).

Has he not been decapitated? Not with a shovel, but with a cross. "God disarmed the evil rulers and authorities. He shamed them publicly by his victory over them on the cross of Christ" (Col. 2:15 NLT).

So how does that leave us? *Confident.* The punch line of the passage is Jesus' power over Satan. One word from Christ, and the demons are swimming with the swine, and the wild man is "clothed and in his right mind" (Mark 5:15). Just one command! No séance needed. No hocus-pocus. No chants were heard or candles lit. Hell is an anthill against heaven's steamroller. Jesus "commands . . . evil spirits, and they obey him" (Mark 1:27 NCV). The snake in the ditch and Lucifer in the pit—both have met their match.

And, yet, both stir up dust long after their defeat. For that reason, though confident, we are still *careful.* For a toothless ol' varmint, Satan sure has some bite! He spooks our work, disrupts our activities, and leaves us thinking twice about where we step. Which we need to do. "Be self-controlled and alert. Your enemy the devil prowls around like a roaring lion looking for someone to devour" (1 Pet. 5:8 NIV). Alertness is needed. Panic is not. The serpent still wiggles and intimidates, but he has no poison. He is defeated, and he knows it! "He knows his time is short" (Rev. 12:12 CEV).

"Greater is He who is in you than he who is in the world" (1 John 4:4). Believe it. Trust the work of your Savior. "Resist the devil and he will flee from you" (James 4:7). In the meantime, the best he can do is squirm.

9

It's Not Up to You

Spiritually Weary People
JOHN 3:1–6

My dog Molly and I aren't getting along. The problem is not her personality. A sweeter mutt you will not find. She sees every person as a friend and every day as a holiday. I have no problem with Molly's attitude. I have a problem with her habits.

Eating scraps out of the trash. Licking dirty plates in the dishwasher. Dropping dead birds on our sidewalk and stealing bones from the neighbor's dog. Shameful! Molly rolls in the grass, chews on her paw, does her business in the wrong places, and, I'm embarrassed to admit, quenches her thirst in the toilet.

Now what kind of behavior is that?

Dog behavior, you reply.

You are right. So right. Molly's problem is not a Molly problem. Molly has a dog problem. It is a dog's nature to do such things. And it is her nature that I wish to change. Not just her behavior, mind you. A canine obedience school can change what she does; I want to go deeper. I want to change who she is.

Here is my idea: a me-to-her transfusion. The deposit of a Max seed in Molly. I want to give her a kernel of human character. As it grew, would she not change? Her human nature would develop, and her dog nature would diminish. We would witness, not just a change of habits, but a change of essence. In time Molly would be less like Molly and more like me, sharing my disgust for trash snacking, potty slurping, and dish licking. She would have a new nature. Why, Denalyn might even let her eat at the table.

You think the plan is crazy? Then take it up with God. The idea is his.

What I would like to do with Molly, God does with us. He changes our nature from the inside out! "I will put a new way of thinking inside you.

I will take out the stubborn hearts of stone from your bodies, and I will give you obedient hearts of flesh. I will put my Spirit inside you and help you live by my rules and carefully obey my laws" (Ezek. 36:26–27 NCV).

God doesn't send us to obedience school to learn new habits; he sends us to the hospital to be given a new heart. Forget training; he gives transplants.

Sound bizarre? Imagine how it sounded to Nicodemus.

There was a man of the Pharisees, named Nicodemus, a ruler of the Jews; this man came to Jesus by night and said to Him, "Rabbi, we know that You have come from God as a teacher; for no one can do these signs that You do unless God is with him." (John 3:1–2)

Nicodemus is impressive. Not only is he one of the six thousand Pharisees, he is a ruler, one of seventy men who serve on the high council. Think of him as a religious blue blood. What the justices are to the Supreme Court, he is to the Law of Moses. Expert. Credentials trail his name like a robe behind a king. Nicodemus, Ph.D., Th.D., M.S., M.Div. Universities want him on their board. Conferences want him on their platform. When it comes to religion, he's loaded. When it comes to life, he's tired.

As a good Jew, he's trying to obey the Talmud. No small endeavor. He has twenty-four chapters of laws regarding the Sabbath alone. Just a sampling:

- Don't eat anything larger than an olive. And if you bite an olive and find it to be rotten, what you spit out is still a part of your allowance.

- You can carry enough ink to draw two letters, but baths aren't allowed for fear of splashing the floor and washing it.

- Tailors can carry no needles.

- Kids can toss no balls. No one can carry a load heavier than a fig, but anything half the weight of a fig can be carried twice.[1]

Whew!

Can a scientist study stars and never weep at their splendor? Dissect a rose and never notice its perfume? Can a theologian study the Law until he decodes the shoe size of Moses but still lack the peace needed for a good night's sleep?

Maybe that's why Nicodemus comes at night. He is tired but can't sleep. Tired of rules and regulations but no rest. Nicodemus is looking for a change. And he has a hunch Jesus can give it.

Though Nicodemus asks no question, Jesus offers him an answer. "Truly, truly, I say to you, unless one is born again he cannot see the kingdom of God" (v. 3).

This is radical language. To see the kingdom of God you need an unprecedented rebirth from God. Nicodemus staggers at the elephantine thought. "How can a man be born when he is old? He cannot enter a second time into his mother's womb and be born, can he?" (v. 4).

Don't you love those last two words? *Can he?* Nicodemus knows that a grown man doesn't reenter the birth canal. There is no Rewind button on the VCR of life . . . is there? We don't get to start over . . . do we? A man can't be born again . . . can he? What causes the question? What makes Nicodemus add those two words? Old Nick should know better. He wasn't born yesterday.

But maybe he wishes he had been. Maybe he wishes he could be born today. Maybe those last two words—"can he?"—emerge from that part of Nicodemus that longs for strength. Youthful vigor. Fresh wind. New legs.

Nicodemus seems to be saying, "Jesus, I've got the spiritual energy of an old mule. How do you expect me to be born again when I can't even remember if figs can be eaten on the Sabbath? I'm an old man. How can a man be born when he is old?" According to Christ, the new birth must come from a new place. "The truth is, no one can enter the Kingdom of God without being born of water and the Spirit. Humans can reproduce only human life, but the Holy Spirit gives new life from heaven" (vv. 5–6 NLT).

Could Jesus be more direct? "*No one* can enter the Kingdom of God without being born of water and the Spirit." You want to go to heaven? Doesn't matter how religious you are or how many rules you keep. You need a new birth; you need to be "born of water and the Spirit."

God gives no sponge baths. He washes us from head to toe. Paul reflected on his conversion and wrote: "He gave us a good bath, and we came out of it new people, washed inside and out by the Holy Spirit" (Titus 3:5 MSG). Your sins stand no chance against the fire hydrant of God's grace.

But more is needed. God is not content to clean you; he indwells you. God deposits within you "His power, which mightily works" (Col. 1:29).

He does not do with you what my dad did with my brother and me. Our high-school car was a '65 Rambler station wagon. The clunker had as much glamour as Forrest Gump: three speed, shift on the column, bench seats covered with plastic, no air conditioning.

And, oh, the engine. Our lawn mower had more power. The car's highest speed, downhill with a tailwind, was fifty miles per hour. To this day I'm convinced that my father (a trained mechanic) searched for the slowest possible car and bought it for us.

When we complained about her pitiful shape, he just smiled and said, "Fix it up." We did the best we could. We cleaned the carpets, sprayed air freshener on the seats, stuck a peace symbol on the back window, and hung Styrofoam dice from the rearview mirror. We removed the hubcaps and spray-painted the rims black. The car looked better, smelled better, but ran the same. Still a clunker—a clean clunker, to be sure—but still a clunker.

Don't for a microsecond think God does this with you. Washing the outside isn't enough for him. He places power on the inside. Better stated, he places *himself* on the inside. This is the part that stunned Nicodemus. Working for God was not new. But God working in him? *I need to chew on that a bit.*

Maybe you do, as well. Are you a Nicodemus? Religious as Saint Peter's Square, but feeling just as old? Pious, but powerless? If so, may I remind you of something?

When you believe in Christ, Christ works a miracle in you. "When you believed in Christ, he identified you as his own by giving you the Holy Spirit" (Eph. 1:13 NLT). You are permanently purified and empowered by God himself. The message of Jesus to the religious person is simple: It's not what you do. It's what I do. I have moved in. And in time you can say with Paul, "I myself no longer live, but Christ lives in me" (Gal. 2:20 NLT). You are no longer a clunker, not even a clean clunker. You are a sleek Indianapolis Motor Speedway racing machine.

If that is true, Max, why do I still sputter? If I'm born again, why do I fall so often?

Why did you fall so often after your first birth? Did you exit the womb wearing cross-trainers? Did you do the two-step on the day of your delivery?

Of course not. And when you started to walk, you fell more than you stood. Should we expect anything different from our spiritual walk?

But I fall so often, I question my salvation. Again, we return to your first birth. Didn't you stumble as you were learning to walk? And when you stumbled, did you question the validity of your physical birth? Did you, as a one-year-old fresh flopped on the floor, shake your head and think, *I have fallen again. I must not be human?*

Of course not. The stumbles of a toddler do not invalidate the act of birth. And the stumbles of a Christian do not annul his spiritual birth.

Do you understand what God has done? He has deposited a Christ seed in you. As it grows, you will change. It's not that sin has no more presence in your life, but rather that sin has no more power over your life. Temptation will pester you, but temptation will not master you. What hope this brings!

Nicodemuses of the world, hear this. It's not up to you! Within you abides a budding power. Trust him!

Think of it this way. Suppose you, for most of your life, have had a heart condition. Your frail pumper restricts your activities. Each morning at work when the healthy employees take the stairs, you wait for the elevator.

But then comes the transplant. A healthy heart is placed within you. After recovery, you return to work and encounter the flight of stairs—the same flight of stairs you earlier avoided. By habit, you start for the elevator. But then you remember. You aren't the same person. You have a new heart. Within you dwells a new power.

Do you live like the old person or the new? Do you count yourself as having a new heart or old? You have a choice to make.

You might say, "I can't climb stairs; I'm too weak." Does your choice negate the presence of a new heart? Dismiss the work of the surgeon? No. Choosing the elevator would suggest only one fact—you haven't learned to trust your new power.

It takes time. But at some point you've got to try those stairs. You've got to test the new ticker. You've got to experiment with the new you. For if you don't, you will run out of steam.

Religious rule keeping can sap your strength. It's endless. There is always another class to attend, Sabbath to obey, Ramadan to observe. No prison is as endless as the prison of perfection. Her inmates find work but never find peace. How could they? They never know when they are finished.

Christ, however, gifts you with a finished work. He fulfilled the law for you. Bid farewell to the burden of religion. Gone is the fear that having done everything, you might not have done enough. You climb the stairs, not by your strength, but his. God pledges to help those who stop trying to help themselves.

"He who began a good work in you will carry it on to completion until the day of Christ Jesus" (Phil. 1:6 NIV). God will do with you what I only dream of doing with Molly. Change you from the inside out. When he is finished, he'll even let you sit at his table.

10

The Trashman

Imperfect People
JOHN 1:29

The woman flops down on the bench and drops her trash bag between her feet. With elbows on knees and cheeks in hands, she stares at the sidewalk. Everything aches. Back. Legs. Neck. Her shoulder is stiff and her hands raw. All because of the sack.

Oh, to be rid of this garbage.

Unbroken clouds form a gray ceiling, gray with a thousand sorrows. Soot-stained buildings cast long shadows, darkening passageways and the people in them. Drizzle chills the air and muddies the rivulets of the street gutters. The woman collects her jacket. A passing car drenches the sack and splashes her jeans. She doesn't move. Too tired.

Her memories of life without the trash are fuzzy. As a child maybe? Her back was straighter, her walk quicker . . . or was it a dream? She doesn't know for sure.

A second car. This one stops and parks. A man steps out. She watches his shoes sink in the slush. From the car he pulls out a trash bag, lumpy with litter. He drapes it over his shoulder and curses the weight.

Neither of them speaks. Who knows if he noticed her. His face seems young, younger than his stooped back. In moments he is gone. Her gaze returns to the pavement.

She never looks at her trash. Early on she did. But what she saw repulsed her, so she's kept the sack closed ever since.

What else can she do? Give it to someone? All have their own.

Here comes a young mother. With one hand she leads a child; with the other she drags her load, bumpy and heavy.

Here comes an old man, face ravined with wrinkles. His trash sack is so long it hits the back of his legs as he walks. He glances at the woman and tries to smile.

What weight would he be carrying? she wonders as he passes.

"Regrets."

She turns to see who spoke. Beside her on the bench sits a man. Tall, with angular cheeks and bright, kind eyes. Like hers, his jeans are mud stained. Unlike hers, his shoulders are straight. He wears a T-shirt and baseball cap. She looks around for his trash but doesn't see it.

He watches the old man disappear as he explains, "As a young father, he worked many hours and neglected his family. His children don't love him. His sack is full, full of regrets."

She doesn't respond. And when she doesn't, he does.

"And yours?"

"Mine?" she asks, looking at him.

"Shame." His voice is gentle, compassionate.

She still doesn't speak, but neither does she turn away.

"Too many hours in the wrong arms. Last year. Last night . . . shame."

She stiffens, steeling herself against the scorn she has learned to expect. As if she needed more shame. Stop him. But how? She awaits his judgment.

But it never comes. His voice is warm and his question honest. "Will you give me your trash?"

Her head draws back. *What can he mean?*

"Give it to me. Tomorrow. At the landfill. Will you bring it?" He rubs a moist smudge from her cheek with his thumb and stands. "Friday. The landfill."

Long after he leaves, she sits, replaying the scene, retouching her cheek. His voice lingers; his invitation hovers. She tries to dismiss his words but can't. How could he know what he knew? And how could he know and still be so kind? The memory sits on the couch of her soul, an uninvited but welcome guest.

That night's sleep brings her summer dreams. A young girl under blue skies and puffy clouds, playing amid wildflowers, skirt twirling. She dreams of running with hands wide open, brushing the tops of sunflowers. She dreams of happy people filling a meadow with laughter and hope.

But when she wakes, the sky is dark, the clouds billowed, and the streets shadowed. At the foot of her bed lies her sack of trash. Hoisting it over her shoulder, she walks out of the apartment and down the stairs and onto the street, still slushy.

It's Friday.

For a time she stands, thinking. First wondering what he meant, then if he really meant it. She sighs. With hope just barely outweighing hopelessness, she turns toward the edge of town. Others are walking in the same direction. The man beside her smells of alcohol. He's slept many nights in his suit. A teenage girl walks a few feet ahead. The woman of shame hurries to catch up. The girl volunteers an answer before the question can be asked: "Rage. Rage at my father. Rage at my mother. I'm tired of anger. He said he'd take it." She motions to the sack. "I'm going to give it to him."

The woman nods, and the two walk together.

The landfill is tall with trash—papers and broken brooms and old beds and rusty cars. By the time they reach the hill, the line to the top is long. Hundreds walk ahead of them. All wait in silence, stunned by what they hear—a scream, a pain-pierced roar that hangs in the air for moments, interrupted only by a groan. Then the scream again.

His.

As they draw nearer, they know why. He kneels before each, gesturing toward the sack, offering a request, then a prayer. "May I have it? And may you never feel it again." Then he bows his head and lifts the sack, emptying its contents upon himself. The selfishness of the glutton, the bitterness of the angry, the possessiveness of the insecure. He feels what they felt. It is as if he'd lied or cheated or cursed his Maker.

Upon her turn, the woman pauses. Hesitates. His eyes compel her to step forward. He reaches for her trash and takes it from her. "You can't live with this," he explains. "You weren't made to." With head down, he empties her shame upon his shoulders. Then looking toward the heavens with tear-flooded eyes, he screams, "I'm sorry!"

"But you did nothing!" she cries.

Still, he sobs as she has sobbed into her pillow a hundred nights. That's when she realizes that his cry is hers. Her shame his.

With her thumb she touches his cheek, and for the first step in a long nighttime, she has no trash to carry.

With the others she stands at the base of the hill and watches as he is buried under a mound of misery. For some time he moans. Then nothing. Just silence.

The people sit among the wrecked cars and papers and discarded stoves and wonder who this man is and what he has done. Like mourners at a wake, they linger. Some share stories. Others say nothing. All cast occasional glances at the landfill. It feels odd, loitering near the heap. But it feels even stranger to think of leaving.

So they stay. Through the night and into the next day. Darkness comes again. A kinship connects them, a kinship through the trashman. Some doze. Others build fires in the metal drums and speak of the sudden abundance of stars in the night sky. By early morning most are asleep.

They almost miss the moment. It is the young girl who sees it. The girl with the rage. She doesn't trust her eyes at first, but when she looks again, she knows.

Her words are soft, intended for no one. "He's standing."

Then aloud, for her friend, "He's standing."

And louder for all, "He's standing!"

She turns; all turn. They see him silhouetted against a golden sun. Standing. Indeed.

Part Two

NO PLACE HE WON'T GO

Charlie was ten. School was out for Christmas, and the family had chosen to spend the holiday in the country. The boy pressed his nose against the bay window of the vacation home and marveled at the British winter. He was happy to trade the blackened streets of London for the cotton-white freshness of snow-covered hills.

His mom invited him to go for a drive, and he quickly accepted. A halcyon moment was in the making. She snaked the car down the twisty road. The tires crunched the snow, and the boy puffed his breath on the window. He was thrilled. The mother, however, was anxious.

Heavy snow began to fall. Visibility lessened. As she took a curve, the car started to slide and didn't stop until it was in a ditch. She tried to drive out. The tires just spun. Little Charlie pushed, and his mom pressed the gas. But no luck. They were stuck. They needed help.

A mile down the road sat a house. Off they went and knocked on the door. "Of course," the woman told them. "Come in; warm yourselves. The phone is yours." She offered tea and cookies and urged them to stay until help arrived.

An ordinary event? Don't suggest that to the woman who opened the door. She has never forgotten that day. She's retold the story a thousand times. And who could blame her? It's not often that royalty appears on your porch.

For the two travelers stranded by the England winter were no less than Queen Elizabeth and the heir to the throne, ten-year-old Charles.[1]

The word on the streets of heaven and the lips of Christians is that something far grander has happened to our world. Royalty has walked down our streets. Heaven's prince has knocked on our door.

His visit, however, was no accident. And he did much more than stay for tea. Wood shops. Wildernesses. Under the water of Jordan. On the water of Galilee. He kept popping up in the oddest places. Places where you'd never expect to spot God.

But, then again, who would have expected to see him at all?

II

He Loves to Be with the Ones He Loves

Every Place

PHILIPPIANS 2:6–7

Holiday time is highway time. Ever since Joseph and Mary packed their bags for Bethlehem, the birth of Jesus has caused people to hit the road. Interestingly, the Christmas trips we take have a lot in common with the maiden voyage of Jesus' folks. We don't see shepherds in the middle of the night, but we have been known to bump into an in-law on the way to the bathroom. We don't sleep in stables, but a living room full of sleeping-bagged cousins might smell like one. And we don't ride donkeys, but six hours in a minivan with four kids might make some moms wish they had one.

"'Tis the season to be traveling." Nothing reveals the true character of family members like a long road trip.

We dads, for example, discover our real identities on the interstate. In the spirit of our Mayflower and Conestoga forefathers, we don't want to stop. Did Lewis and Clark ask for directions? Did the pioneers spend the night at a Holiday Inn? Did Joseph allow Mary to stroll through a souvenir shop in Bethlehem to buy an ornament for the tree?

By no means. We men have a biblical mandate to travel far and fast, stopping only for gasoline.

Wives, however, know the real reason we husbands love to drive: the civil war in the backseat.

Did you know sociologists have proven that backseats have a wolfman impact on kids? Fangs, growls, claws. Social skills disappear into the same black hole as dropped French fries. Sojourning siblings are simply incapable of normal human conversation. If one child says, "I like that song," you might expect the other to say, "That's nice." He won't. Instead, he will reply, "It stinks, and so do your shoes."

83

The best advice for traveling with children is to be thankful they aren't teenagers. Teens are crawl-under-the-car humiliated by their dads. They are embarrassed by what we say, think, wear, eat, and sing. So, dads, if you seek peaceful passage (and if you ever want to see your unborn grandchildren), don't smile in a restaurant, don't breathe, and don't sing with the window down or up.

Holiday travel. It isn't easy. Then why do we do it? Why cram the trunks and endure the airports? You know the answer. We love to be with the ones we love.

The four-year-old running up the sidewalk into the arms of Grandpa.

The cup of coffee with Mom before the rest of the house awakes.

That moment when, for a moment, everyone is quiet as we hold hands around the table and thank God for family and friends and pumpkin pie.

We love to be with the ones we love.

May I remind you? So does God. He loves to be with the ones he loves. How else do you explain what he did? Between him and us there was a distance—a great span. And he couldn't bear it. He couldn't stand it. So he did something about it.

Before coming to the earth, "Christ himself was like God in everything. . . . But he gave up his place with God and made himself nothing. He was born to be a man and became like a servant" (Phil. 2:6–7 NCV).

Why? Why did Jesus travel so far?

I was asking myself that question when I spotted the squirrels outside my window. A family of black-tailed squirrels has made its home amid the roots of the tree north of my office. We've been neighbors for three years now. They watch me peck the keyboard. I watch them store their nuts and climb the trunk. We're mutually amused. I could watch them all day. Sometimes I do.

But I've never considered becoming one of them. The squirrel world holds no appeal to me. Who wants to sleep next to a hairy rodent with beady eyes? (No comments from you wives who feel you already do.) Give up the Rocky Mountains, bass fishing, weddings, and laughter for a hole in the ground and a diet of dirty nuts? Count me out.

But count Jesus in. What a world he left. Our classiest mansion would be a tree trunk to him. Earth's finest cuisine would be walnuts on heaven's table. And the idea of becoming a squirrel with claws and tiny teeth and a furry tail? It's nothing compared to God becoming a one-celled embryo and entering the womb of Mary.

But he did. The God of the universe kicked against the wall of a womb, was born into the poverty of a peasant, and spent his first night in the feed trough of a cow. "The Word became flesh and lived among us" (John 1:14 NRSV). The God of the universe left the glory of heaven and moved into the neighborhood. Our neighborhood! Who could have imagined he would do such a thing.

Why? He loves to be with the ones he loves.

Dr. Maxwell Maltz tells a remarkable story of a love like this. A man had been injured in a fire while attempting to save his parents from a burning house. He couldn't get to them. They perished. His face was burned and disfigured. He mistakenly interpreted his pain as God's punishment. The man wouldn't let anyone see him—not even his wife.

She went to Dr. Maltz, a plastic surgeon, for help. He told the woman not to worry. "I can restore his face."

The wife was unenthused. Her husband had repeatedly refused any help. She knew he would again.

Then why her visit? "I want you to disfigure my face so I can be like him! If I can share in his pain, then maybe he will let me back into his life."

Dr. Maltz was shocked. He denied her request but was so moved by this woman's love that he went to speak with her husband. Knocking on the man's bedroom door, he called loudly, "I'm a plastic surgeon, and I want you to know that I can restore your face."

No response.

"Please come out."

Again there was no answer.

Still speaking through the door, Dr. Maltz told the man of his wife's proposal. "She wants me to disfigure her face, to make her face like yours in the hope that you will let her back into your life. That's how much she loves you."

There was a brief moment of silence, and then, ever so slowly, the doorknob began to turn.[1]

The way the woman felt for her husband is the way God feels about us. But he did more than make the offer. He took on our face, our disfigurement. He became like us. Just look at the places he was willing to go: feed troughs, carpentry shops, badlands, and cemeteries. The places he went to reach us show how far he will go to touch us.

He loves to be with the ones he loves.

12

What's It Like?

Inward Places

LUKE 1:38

Some things only a mom can do.

Only a mother can powder a baby's behind with one hand and hold the phone with the other. Only a mom can discern which teen is entering the door just by the sound of the key in the lock. Only a mom can spend a day wiping noses, laundering enough socks for the Yankees, balancing a checkbook down to $1.27, and still mean it when she thanks God for her kids. Only a mom.

Some things only a mom can fix. Like Hamburger Helper without the hamburger. Like the cabinet door her husband couldn't and his bruised ego when he found out that she could. Broken shoelace? Broken heart? Breaking out on your face? Breaking up with your sweetheart? Moms can handle that. Some things only a mom can fix.

Some things only a mom can know. The time it takes to drive from piano lesson to Little League practice? She knows. How many pizzas you need for a middle school sleepover? Mom knows. How many Weight Watcher points are left in the day and days are left in the semester? Mom can tell you. She knows.

We men usually don't. The kids are usually clueless. Moms are a breed apart. The rest of us can only wonder, only ponder. We can only ask,

MOM, WHAT'S IT LIKE?

When you felt the foot within your womb,
    when the infant cry first filled the room . . .
        to think that you and heaven just circled the moon . . .
What's that like?

89

And the day the bus pulled to a stop
    and you zipped the jacket up to the top
    and placed a kiss on a five-year-old's cheek
    and waved good-bye, then saw the trike—
    silent and still—
What's it like?

The first time you noticed his voice was deep.
The first time she asked if you were asleep
    and wanted to know when love was real.
And you told her. How did you feel?

Then the candles were lit.
She came down the aisle.
Did you weep? Did you smile?
And when your child with child told you the news,
    and in the quiet of the corner asked for clues.
"Mom," she whispered, "what's it like?"

What you told her would you tell us? Indeed, what is it like?

If we've ever wondered such thoughts about mothers, how much more have we wondered them about the most famous mother of all: Mary. To bear a baby is one thing, but to carry God? What is that like?

The virgin birth is more, much more, than a Christmas story; it is a picture of how close Christ will come to you. The first stop on his itinerary was a womb. Where will God go to touch the world? Look deep within Mary for an answer.

Better still, look deep within yourself. What he did with Mary, he offers to us! He issues a Mary-level invitation to all his children. "If you'll let me, I'll move in!"

Proliferating throughout Scripture is a preposition that leaves no doubt— the preposition *in.* Jesus lives *in* his children.

To his apostles, Christ declared, "I am *in* you" (John 14:20 NCV, emphasis mine).

Paul's prayer for the Ephesians was "that Christ may dwell *in* your hearts through faith" (Eph. 3:17 NIV, emphasis mine).

What is the mystery of the gospel? "Christ *in* you, the hope of glory" (Col. 1:27 NIV, emphasis mine).

John was clear, "Those who obey his commands live *in* him, and he *in* them" (1 John 3:24 NIV, emphasis mine).

And the sweetest invitation from Christ? "Here I am! I stand at the door and knock. If anyone hears my voice and opens the door, I will come *in* and eat with him, and he with me" (Rev. 3:20 NIV, emphasis mine).

Christ grew in Mary until he had to come out. Christ will grow in you until the same occurs. He will come out in your speech, in your actions, in your decisions. Every place you live will be a Bethlehem, and every day you live will be a Christmas. You, like Mary, will deliver Christ into the world.

God *in* us! Have we sounded the depth of this promise?

God was *with* Adam and Eve, walking with them in the cool of the evening.

God was *with* Abraham, even calling the patriarch his friend.

God was *with* Moses and the children of Israel. Parents could point their children to the fire by night and cloud by day; *God is with us,* they could assure.

Between the cherubim of the ark, in the glory of the temple, God was *with* his people. He was *with* the apostles. Peter could touch God's beard. John could watch God sleep. Multitudes could hear his voice. God was *with* them!

But he is *in* you. You are a modern-day Mary. Even more so. He was a fetus in her, but he is a force in you. He will do what you cannot. Imagine a million dollars being deposited into your checking account. To any observer you look the same, except for the goofy smile, but are you? Not at all! With God *in* you, you have a million resources that you did not have before!

Can't stop drinking? Christ can. And he lives within you.

Can't stop worrying? Christ can. And he lives within you.

Can't forgive the jerk, forget the past, or forsake your bad habits? Christ can! And he lives within you.

Paul knew this. "For this purpose also I labor, striving according to His power, which mightily works with *in* me" (Col. 1:29, emphasis mine).

Like Mary, you and I are indwelt by Christ.

Find that hard to believe? How much more did Mary? The line beneath her picture in the high-school annual did not read, "Aspires to be the mother of God." No. No one was more surprised by this miracle than she was.

And no one was more passive than she was. God did everything. Mary didn't volunteer to help. What did she have to offer? Advice? "From my perspective, a heavenly choir would add a nice touch." Yeah, right. She offered no assistance.

And she offered no resistance. She could have. "Who am I to have God in my womb? I'm not good enough," she could have said. Or, "I've got other plans. I don't have time for God in my life."

But Mary didn't say such words. Instead, she said, "Behold, the bond-slave of the Lord; may it be done to me according to your word" (Luke 1:38). If Mary is our measure, God seems less interested in talent and more interested in trust.

Unlike her, we tend to assist God, assuming our part is as important as his. Or we resist, thinking we are too bad or too busy. Yet when we assist or resist, we miss God's great grace. We miss out on the reason we were placed on earth—to be so pregnant with heaven's child that he lives through us. To be so full of him that we could say with Paul, "It is no longer I who live, but Christ lives in me" (Gal. 2:20).

What would *that* be like? To have a child within is a miracle, but to have Christ within?

> To have my voice, but him speaking.
> My steps, but Christ leading.
> My heart, but his love beating
> in me, through me, with me.
> What's it like to have Christ on the inside?
>
> To tap his strength when mine expires
> or feel the force of heaven's fires
> raging, purging wrong desires.
> Could Christ become my self entire?
>
> So much him, so little me
> that in my eyes it's him they see.
> What's it like to a Mary be?
> No longer I, but Christ in me.

13

A Cure for the Common Life

Ordinary Places

MARK 6:3

You awoke today to a common day. No butler drew your bath. No maid laid out your clothes. Your eggs weren't Benedict, and your orange juice wasn't fresh squeezed. But that's OK; there's nothing special about the day. It's not your birthday or Christmas; it's like every other day. A common day.

So you went to the garage and climbed into your common car. You once read that children of the queen never need to drive. You've been told of executives and sheiks who are helicoptered to their offices. As for you, a stretch limo took you to your wedding reception, but since then it's been sedans and minivans. Common cars.

Common cars that take you to your common job. You take it seriously, but you would never call it extraordinary. You're not clearing your calendar for Jay Leno or making time to appear before Congress. You're just making sure you get your work done before the six o'clock rush turns the Loop into a parking lot.

Get caught in the evening traffic, and be ready to wait in line. The line at the freeway on-ramp. The line at the grocery or the line at the gas station. If you were the governor or had an Oscar on your mantel, you might bypass the crowds. But you aren't. You are common.

You lead a common life. Punctuated by occasional weddings, job transfers, bowling trophies, and graduations—a few highlights—but mainly the day-to-day rhythm that you share with the majority of humanity.

And, as a result, you could use a few tips. You need to know how to succeed at being common. Commonhood has its perils, you know. A face in the crowd can feel lost in the crowd. You tend to think you are unproductive, wondering if you'll leave any lasting contribution. And you can feel insignificant. Do commoners rate in heaven? Does God love common people?

God answers these questions in a most uncommon fashion. If the word *common* describes you, take heart—you're in fine company. It also describes Christ.

Christ common? Come on. Since when is walking on water "common"? Speaking to the dead "common"? Being raised from the dead "common"? Can we call the life of Christ "common"?

Nine-tenths of it we can. When you list the places Christ lived, draw a circle around the town named Nazareth—a single-camel map dot on the edge of boredom. For thirty of his thirty-three years, Jesus lived a common life. Aside from that one incident in the temple at the age of twelve, we have no record of what he said or did for the first thirty years he walked on this earth.

Were it not for a statement in Mark's gospel, we would not know anything about Jesus' early adult life. It's not much, but just enough thread to weave a thought or two for those who suffer from the common life. If you chum with NBA stars and subscribe to *Yachting Monthly,* you can tune out. If you wouldn't know what to say to NBA stars and have never heard of *Yachting Monthly,* then perk up. Here is the verse:

"Is not this the carpenter?" (Mark 6:3).

(Told you it wasn't much.) Jesus' neighbors spoke those words. Amazed at his latter-life popularity, they asked, "Is this the same guy who fixed my roof?"

Note what his neighbors did not say:

"Is not this the carpenter who owes me money?"

"Is not this the carpenter who swindled my father?"

"Is not this the carpenter who never finished my table?"

No, these words were never said. The lazy have a hard time hiding in a small town. Hucksters move from city to city to survive. Jesus didn't need to. Need a plow repaired? Christ could do it. In need of a new yoke? "My neighbor is a carpenter, and he will give you a fair price." The job may have been common, but his diligence was not. Jesus took his work seriously.

And the town may have been common, but his attention to it was not. The city of Nazareth sits on a summit. Certainly no Nazarene boy could resist an occasional hike to the crest to look out over the valley beneath. Sitting six hundred feet above the level of the sea, the young Jesus could examine this world he had made. Mountain flowers in the spring. Cool sunsets. Pelicans winging their way along the streams of Kishon to the Sea of Galilee. Thyme-besprinkled turf at his feet. Fields and fig trees in the distance. Do you suppose moments here inspired these words later? "Observe how the lilies of the field grow" (Matt. 6:28) or "Look at the birds of the air" (Matt. 6:26). The words of Jesus the rabbi were born in the thoughts of Jesus the boy.

To the north of Nazareth lie the wood-crowned hills of Naphtali. Conspicuous on one of them was the village of Safed, known in the region as "the city set upon the hill."[1] Was Jesus thinking of Safed when he said, "A city set on a hill cannot be hidden" (Matt. 5:14)?

The maker of yokes later explained, "My yoke is easy" (Matt. 11:30). The one who brushed his share of sawdust from his eyes would say, "Why do you look at the speck that is in your brother's eye, but do not notice the log that is in your own eye?" (Matt. 7:3).

He saw how a seed on the path took no root (Luke 8:5) and how a mustard seed produced a great tree (Matt. 13:31–32). He remembered the red sky at morning (Matt. 16:2) and the lightning in the eastern sky (Matt. 24:27). Jesus listened to his common life.

Are you listening to yours? Rain pattering against the window. Silent snow in April. The giggle of a baby on a crowded plane. Seeing a sunrise while the world sleeps. Are these not personal epistles? Can't God speak through a Monday commute or a midnight diaper change? Take notes on your life.

> There is no event so commonplace but that God is present within it, always hiddenly, always leaving you room to recognize him or not recognize him. . . . See [your life] for the fathomless mystery that it is. In the boredom and pain of it no less than in the excitement and gladness: touch, taste, and smell your way to the holy and hidden heart of it because in the last analysis all moments are key moments, and life itself is grace.[2]

Next time your life feels ordinary, take your cue from Christ. Pay attention to your work and your world. Jesus' obedience began in a small town carpentry shop. His uncommon approach to his common life groomed him for his uncommon call. "When Jesus entered public life he was about thirty years old" (Luke 3:23 MSG). In order to enter public life, you have to leave private life. In order for Jesus to change the world, he had to say good-bye to *his* world.

He had to give Mary a kiss. Have a final meal in the kitchen, a final walk through the streets. Did he ascend one of the hills of Nazareth and think of the day he would ascend the hill near Jerusalem?

He knew what was going to happen. "God chose him for this purpose long before the world began" (1 Pet. 1:20 NLT). Every ounce of suffering had been scripted—it just fell to him to play the part.

Not that he had to. Nazareth was a cozy town. Why not build a carpentry business? Keep his identity a secret? Return in the era of guillotines or electric chairs, and pass on the cross. To be forced to die is one thing, but to willingly take up your own cross is something else.

Alan and Penny McIlroy can tell you. The fact that they have two adopted children is commendable but not uncommon. The fact that they have adopted special needs children is significant but not unique. It's the severity of the health problems that sets this story apart.

Saleena is a cocaine baby. Her birth mother's overdose left Saleena unable to hear, see, speak, or move. Penny and Alan adopted her at seven weeks. The doctor gave her a year. She's lived for six.

As Penny introduced me to Saleena, she ruffled her hair and squeezed her cheeks, but Saleena didn't respond. She never does. Barring a miracle, she never will. Neither will her sister. "This is Destiny," Penny told me. In the adjacent bed one-year-old Destiny lay, motionless and vegetative. Penny will never hear Destiny's voice. Alan will never know Saleena's kiss. They'll never hear their daughters sing in a choir, never see them walk across the stage. They'll bathe them, change them, adjust their feeding tubes, and rub their limp limbs, but barring God's intervention, this mom and dad will never hear more than we heard that afternoon— gurgled breathing. "I need to suction Saleena's nose," Penny said to me. "You might want to leave."[3]

I did, and as I did, I wondered, what kind of love is this? What kind of love adopts disaster? What kind of love looks into the face of children, knowing full well the weight of their calamity, and says, "I'll take them"?

When you come up with a word for such a love, give it to Christ. For the day he left Nazareth is the day he declared his devotion for you and me. We were just as helpless, in a spiritually vegetative state from sin. According to Peter, our lives were "dead-end, empty-headed" (1 Pet. 1:18 MSG). But God, "immense in mercy and with an incredible love . . . embraced us. He took our sin-dead lives and made us alive in Christ. He did all this on his own, with no help from us!" (Eph. 2:4–5 MSG).

Jesus left Nazareth in pursuit of the spiritual Saleenas and Destinys of the world and brought us to life.

Perhaps we aren't so common after all.

14

Oh, to Be DTP-Free!

Religious Places

LUKE 2:41–49

Remember when only people contracted viruses? Remember when terms like *parasite* and *worm* were applied to living organisms and little brothers? Remember when viral infections were treated by doctors and *quarantine* meant the isolation of diseased people and pets?

No longer. Nowadays computers get sick. Preparation of this chapter would have begun several hours earlier had not a biohazardous, chemical-warfare-type warning put a freeze on my keyboard. "Open nothing! Your computer may have a virus!" I half expected Centers for Disease Control agents wearing radioactive gear to rush in, cover me, and run out with my laptop.

They didn't, but a computer doctor did. He installed an antivirus program that protects the machine against 60,959 viruses.

I started to ask if Ebola was one, but I didn't. I did learn that hundreds of thousands of viruses have been created, I'm assuming by the same folks who spray graffiti on buildings and loosen salt shakers at restaurants. Troublemakers who Trojan horse their way into your computer and gobble your data like a Pac-Man. I told the computer guy I'd never seen anything like it.

Later I realized I had. Indeed, a computer virus is a common cold compared to the Chernobyl-level attack you and I must face. Think of your mind as a computer made to store and process massive amounts of data (no comments about your neighbor's hard-drive capacity, please). Think of your strengths as software. Pianists are loaded with music programs. Accountants seem to be born with spreadsheet capacity. Fun lovers come with games installed. We are different, but we each have a computer and software, and, sadly, we have viruses. You and I are infected by destructive thoughts.

Computer viruses have names like Klez, Anna Kournikova, and ILOVEYOU. Mental viruses are known as anxiety, bitterness, anger, guilt, shame, greed, and insecurity. They worm their way into your system and diminish, even disable, your mind. We call these DTPs: destructive thought patterns. (Actually, I'm the only one to call them DTPs.)

Do you have any DTPs?

When you see the successful, are you jealous?

When you see the struggler, are you pompous?

If someone gets on your bad side, is that person as likely to get on your good side as I am to win the Tour-de-France?

Ever argue with someone in your mind? Rehash or rehearse your hurts? Do you assume the worst about the future?

If so, you suffer from DTPs.

What would your world be like without them? Had no dark or destructive thought ever entered your mind, how would you be different? Suppose you could relive your life sans any guilt, lust, vengeance, insecurity, or fear. Never wasting mental energy on gossip or scheming. Would you be different?

What would you have that you don't have? (Suggested answers found on page 107.)

What would you have done that you haven't done? (Suggested answers found on page 107.)

Oh, to be DTP-free. No energy lost, no time wasted. Wouldn't such a person be energetic and wise? A lifetime of healthy and holy thoughts would render anyone a joyful genius.

But where would you find such an individual? An uninfected computer can be bought—but an uninfected person? Impossible. Trace a computer virus back to a hacker. Trace our mental viruses back to the fall of the first man, Adam. Because of sin, our minds are full of dark thoughts. "Although they knew God, they neither glorified him as God nor gave thanks to him, but their thinking became futile and their foolish hearts were darkened. Although they claimed to be wise, they became fools" (Rom. 1:21–22 NIV).

Blame DTPs on sin. Sin messes with the mind. But what if the virus never entered? Suppose a person never opened Satan's e-mails? What would that person be like?

A lot like the twelve-year-old boy seated in the temple of Jerusalem. Though he was beardless and unadorned, this boy's thoughts were profound. Just ask the theologians with whom he conversed. Luke gives this account:

> [His parents] found Him in the temple, sitting in the midst of the teachers, both listening to them and asking them questions. And all who heard Him were amazed at His understanding and His answers. (Luke 2:46–47)

For three days Joseph and Mary were separated from Jesus. The temple was the last place they thought to search. But it was the first place Jesus went. He didn't go to a cousin's house or a buddy's playground. Jesus sought the place of godly thinking and, in doing so, inspires us to do the same. By the time Joseph and Mary located their son, he had confounded the most learned men in the temple. This boy did not think like a boy.

Why? What made Jesus different? The Bible is silent about his IQ. When it comes to the RAM size of his mental computer, we are told nothing. But when it comes to his purity of mind, we are given this astounding claim: Christ "knew no sin" (2 Cor. 5:21). Peter says Jesus "did no sin, neither was guile found in his mouth" (1 Pet. 2:22 KJV). John lived next to him for three years and concluded, "In Him there is no sin" (1 John 3:5).

Spotless was his soul, and striking was the witness of those who knew him. His fleshly brother James called Christ "the righteous man" (James 5:6). Pilate could find no fault in him (John 18:38). Judas confessed that he, in betraying Christ, betrayed innocent blood (Matt. 27:4). Even the demons declared his unique status: "I know who you are—the Holy One of God!" (Luke 4:34 NIV).

The loudest testimony to his perfection was the silence that followed this question. When his accusers called him a servant of Satan, Jesus demanded to see their evidence. "Which one of you convicts Me of sin?" he dared (John 8:46). Ask my circle of friends to point out my sin, and watch the hands shoot up. When those who knew Jesus were asked this same question, no one spoke. Christ was followed by disciples, analyzed by crowds, criticized by family, and scrutinized by enemies, yet not one person would remember him committing even one sin. He was never found in the wrong place. Never said the wrong word. Never acted the wrong way. He never sinned. Not that he wasn't tempted, mind you. He was "tempted in all things as we are, yet without sin" (Heb. 4:15).

Lust wooed him. Greed lured him. Power called him. Jesus—the human— was tempted. But Jesus—the holy God—resisted. Contaminated e-mail came his way, but he resisted the urge to open it.

The word *sinless* has never survived cohabitation with another person. Those who knew Christ best, however, spoke of his purity in unison and with conviction. And because he was sinless, his mind was stainless. DTP-less. No wonder people were "amazed at his teaching" (Mark 1:22 NCV). His mind was virus-free.

But does this matter? Does the perfection of Christ affect me? If he were a distant Creator, the answer would be no. But since he is a next door Savior, the reply is a supersized yes!

Remember the twelve-year-old boy in the temple? The one with sterling thoughts and a Teflon mind? Guess what. That is God's goal for you! You are made to be like Christ! God's priority is that you be "transformed by the renewing of your mind" (Rom. 12:2 NIV). You may have been born virus-prone, but you don't have to live that way. There is hope for your head! Are you a worrywart? Don't have to be one forever. Guilt plagued and shame stained? Prone to anger? Jealousy? God can take care of that. God can change your mind.

If ever there was a DTP candidate, it was George. Abandoned by his father, orphaned by his mother, the little boy was shuffled from foster parent to homelessness and back several times. A sitting duck for bitterness and anger, George could have spent his life getting even. But he didn't. He didn't because Mariah Watkins taught him to think good thoughts.

The needs of each attracted the other—Mariah, a childless washer-woman, and George, a homeless orphan. When Mariah discovered the young boy sleeping in her barn, she took him in. Not only that, she took care of him, took him to church, and helped him find his way to God. When George left Mariah's home, among his few possessions was a Bible she'd given him. By the time he left her home, she had left her mark.[1]

And by the time George left this world, he had left his.

George—George Washington Carver—is a father of modern agriculture.

History credits him with more than three hundred products extracted from peanuts alone. The once-orphaned houseguest of Mariah Watkins became the friend of Henry Ford, Mahatma Gandhi, and three presidents. He entered his laboratory every morning with the prayer "Open thou mine eyes, that I may behold wondrous things out of thy law."[2]

God answers such prayers. He changes the man by changing the mind. And how does it happen? By doing what you are doing right now. Considering the glory of Christ. "But we all, with unveiled face, beholding as in a mirror the glory of the Lord, are being transformed into the same image from glory to glory, just as from the Lord, the Spirit" (2 Cor. 3:18).

To behold him is to become like him. As Christ dominates your thoughts, he changes you from one degree of glory to another until—hang on!—you are ready to live with him.

Heaven is the land of sinless minds. Virus-free thinking. Absolute trust. No fear or anger. Shame and second-guessing are practices of a prior life. Heaven will be wonderful, not because the streets are gold, but because our thoughts will be pure.

So what are you waiting on? Apply God's antivirus. "Set your mind on the things above, not on the things that are on earth" (Col. 3:2). Give him your best thoughts, and see if he doesn't change your mind.

Answers to questions on page 104:

More sleep, joy, and peace

Hugged kids more, loved spouse better, invented computer-virus killer, and traveled to Paris to watch Max win the Tour-de-France

15

Tire Kicker to Car Buyer

Unexpected Places
MATTHEW 3:13–17

No one pays him special attention. Not that they should. Nothing in his appearance separates him from the crowd. Like the rest, he is standing in line, waiting his turn. The coolness of the mud feels nice between his toes, and the occasional lap of water is welcome on his feet. He, like the others, can hear the voice of the preacher in the distance.

Between baptisms, John the Baptist is prone to preach. Impetuous. Fiery. Ferocious. Fearless. Bronzed face, unshorn locks. His eyes are as wild as the countryside from which he came. His whole presence is a sermon— a voice, "a voice of one calling in the desert, 'Prepare the way for the Lord'" (Luke 3:4 NIV).

He stands waist-deep in the cobalt-colored Jordan. He makes a wardrobe out of camel's hair, a meal out of bugs, and, most important, he makes a point of calling all people to the water. "He went into all the country around the Jordan, preaching a baptism of repentance for the forgiveness of sins" (Luke 3:3 NIV).

Baptism wasn't a new practice. It was a required rite for any Gentile seeking to become a Jew. Baptism was for the moldy, second-class, unchosen people, not the clean, top-of-the-line class favorites—the Jews. Herein lies the rub. John refuses to delineate between Jew and Gentile. In his book, every heart needs a detail job.

Every heart, that is, except one. That's why John is stunned when that one wades into the river.

But John didn't want to baptize him. "I am the one who needs to be baptized by you," he said, "so why are you coming to me?"

But Jesus said, "It must be done, because we must do everything that is right." So then John baptized him.

After his baptism, as Jesus came up out of the water, the heavens were opened and he saw the Spirit of God descending like a dove and settling on him. And a voice from heaven said, "This is my beloved Son, and I am fully pleased with him." (Matt. 3:14–17 NLT)

John's reluctance is understandable. A baptismal ceremony is an odd place to find the Son of God. He should be the baptizer not the baptizee. Why would Christ want to be baptized? If baptism was, and is, for the confessed sinner, how do we explain the immersion of history's only sinless soul?

You'll find the answer in the pronouns: "Jesus answered, 'For now this is how it should be, because *we* must do all that God wants *us* to do'" (Matt. 3:15 CEV, emphasis mine).

Who is "we"? Jesus and us. Why does Jesus include himself? It's easy to understand why you and I and John the Baptist and the crowds at the creek have to do what God says. But Jesus? Why would he need to be baptized?

Here's why: He did for us what I did for one of my daughters in the shop at New York's La Guardia Airport. The sign above the ceramic pieces read Do Not Touch. But the wanting was stronger than the warning, and she touched. And it fell. By the time I looked up, ten-year-old Sara was holding the two pieces of a New York City skyline. Next to her was an unhappy store manager. Over them both was the written rule. Between them hung a nervous silence. My daughter had no money. He had no mercy. So I did what dads do. I stepped in. "How much do *we* owe you?" I asked.

How was it that I owed anything? Simple. She was my daughter. And since she could not pay, I did.

Since you and I cannot pay, Christ did. We've broken so much more than souvenirs. We've broken commandments, promises, and, worst of all, we've broken God's heart.

But Christ sees our plight. With the law on the wall and shattered commandments on the floor, he steps near (like a neighbor) and offers a gift (like a Savior).

What do we owe? We owe God a perfect life. Perfect obedience to every command. Not just the command of baptism, but the commands of humility, honesty, integrity. We can't deliver. Might as well charge us for the property of Manhattan. But Christ can and he did. His plunge into the Jordan is a picture of his plunge into our sin. His baptism announces, "Let me pay."

Your baptism responds, "You bet I will." He publicly offers. We publicly accept. We "became part of Christ when we were baptized" (Rom. 6:3 NCV). In baptism we identify with Christ. We go from tire kicker to car buyer. We step out of the shadows, point in his direction, and announce, "I'm with him."

I used to do this at the drive-in movie theater.

Remember drive-in movies? (Kids, ask a grownup.) The one in Andrews, Texas, had a Friday night special—a carload for the price of the driver. Whether the car carried one passenger or a dozen, the price was the same. We often opted for the dozen route. The law would not allow us to do today what we did then. Shoulders squished. Little guy on the big guy's lap. The ride was miserable, but the price was right. When the person at the ticket window looked in, we pointed to the driver and said, "We're with him."

God doesn't tell you to climb into Christ's car; he tells you to climb into Christ! "There is now no condemnation for those who are in Christ Jesus" (Rom. 8:1 NIV). He is your vehicle! Baptism celebrates your decision to take a seat. "For all of you who were baptized *into* Christ have clothed yourselves with Christ" (Gal. 3:27, emphasis mine). We are not saved by the act, but the act demonstrates the way we are saved. We are given credit for a perfect life we did not lead—indeed, a life we could never lead.

We are given a gift similar to the one Billy Joel gave his daughter. On her twelfth birthday she was in New York City, and the pop musician was in Los Angeles. He phoned her that morning, apologizing for his absence, but told her to expect the delivery of a large package before the end of the day. The daughter answered the doorbell that evening to find a seven-foot-tall, brightly wrapped box. She tore it open, and out stepped her father, fresh off the plane from the West Coast.

Can you imagine her surprise?[1]

Perhaps you can. Your gift came in the flesh too.

16

The Long, Lonely Winter

Wilderness Places

LUKE 4:1–13

The wilderness of the desert. Parched ground. Sharp rocks. Shifting sand. Burning sun. Thorns that cut. A miraging oasis. Wavy horizons ever beyond reach. This is the wilderness of the desert.

The wilderness of the soul. Parched promises. Sharp words. Shifting commitments. Burning anger. Rejections that cut. Miraging hope. Distant solutions ever beyond reach. This is the wilderness of the soul.

Some of you know the first. All of you know the second. Jesus, however, knew both.

With skin still moist with Jordan water, he turned away from food and friends and entered the country of hyenas, lizards, and vultures. He was "led around by the Spirit in the wilderness for forty days, being tempted by the devil. And He ate nothing during those days, and when they had ended, He became hungry" (Luke 4:1–2).

The wilderness was not a typical time for Jesus. Normalcy was left at the Jordan and would be rediscovered in Galilee. The wilderness was and is atypical. A dark parenthesis in the story of life. A fierce season of face-to-face encounters with the devil.

You needn't journey to Israel to experience the wilderness. A cemetery will do just fine. So will a hospital. Grief can lead you into the desert. So can divorce or debt or depression.

Received word this morning of a friend who, thinking he was cancer-free, is going back for chemotherapy. Wilderness. Ran into a fellow at lunch who once talked to me about his tough marriage. Asked him how it was going. "It's going," he shrugged. Wilderness. Opened an e-mail from an acquaintance who is spending her summer at the house of her dying mother. She and hospice and death. Waiting. In the wilderness.

You can often chalk up wilderness wanderings to transition. Jesus entered the Jordan River a carpenter and exited a Messiah. His baptism flipped a breaker switch.

Been through any transitions lately? A transfer? Job promotion? Job demotion? A new house? If so, be wary. The wilderness might be near.

How do you know when you're in one?

You are lonely. Whether in fact or in feeling, no one can help, understand, or rescue you.

And your struggle seems endless. In the Bible the number forty is associated with lengthy battles. Noah faced rain for forty days. Moses faced the desert for forty years. Jesus faced temptation for forty nights. Please note, he didn't face temptation for one day out of forty. Jesus was "in the wilderness for forty days, being tempted by the devil" (vv. 1–2). The battle wasn't limited to three questions. Jesus spent a month and ten days slugging it out with Satan. The wilderness is a long, lonely winter.

Doctor after doctor. Résumé after résumé. Diaper after diaper. Zoloft after Zoloft. Heartache after heartache. The calendar is stuck in February, and you're stuck in South Dakota, and you can't even remember what spring smells like.

One more symptom of the badlands: You think the unthinkable. Jesus did. Wild possibilities crossed his mind. Teaming up with Satan? Opting to be a dictator and not a Savior? Torching Earth and starting over on Pluto? We don't know what he thought. We just know this. He was tempted. And "one is tempted when he is carried away and enticed by his own lust" (James 1:14). Temptation "carries" you and "entices" you. What was unimaginable prior to the wilderness becomes possible in it. A tough marriage can make a good man look twice at the wrong woman. Extended sickness makes even the stoutest soul consider suicide. Stress makes the smokiest nightclub smell sweet. The wilderness weakens resolve.

For that reason, the wilderness is the maternity ward for addictions. Binge eating, budget-busting gambling, excessive drinking, pornography—all short-term solutions to deep-seated problems. Typically they have no appeal, but in the wilderness you give thought to the unthinkable.

Jesus did. Jesus was "tempted by the devil" (Luke 4:2). Satan's words, if for but a moment, gave him pause. He may not have eaten the bread, but he stopped long enough in front of the bakery to smell it. Christ knows the wilderness. More than you might imagine. After all, going there was his idea.

Don't blame this episode on Satan. He didn't come to the desert looking for Jesus. Jesus went to the badlands looking for him. "The Spirit led Jesus into the desert *to be tempted* by the devil" (Matt. 4:1 NCV, emphasis mine). Heaven orchestrated this date. How do we explain this? The list of surprising places grows again. If Jesus in the womb and the Jordan waters doesn't stun you, Jesus in the wilderness will. Why did Jesus go to the desert?

Does the word *rematch* mean anything to you? For the second time in history an unfallen mind will be challenged by the fallen angel. The Second Adam has come to succeed where the first Adam failed. Jesus, however, faces a test far more severe. Adam was tested in a garden; Christ is in a stark wasteland. Adam faced Satan on a full stomach; Christ is in the midst of a fast. Adam had a companion: Eve. Christ has no one. Adam was challenged to remain sinless in a sinless world. Christ, on the other hand, is challenged to remain sinless in a sin-ridden world.

Stripped of any aid or excuses, Christ dares the devil to climb into the ring. "You've been haunting my children since the beginning. See what you can do with me." And Satan does. For forty days the two go toe-to-toe. The Son of heaven is tempted but never wavers, struck but never struck down. He succeeds where Adam failed. This victory, according to Paul, is a huge victory for us all. "Here it is in a nutshell: Just as one person did it wrong and got us in all this trouble with sin and death, another person did it right and got us out of it" (Rom. 5:18 MSG).

Christ continues his role as your proxy, your stand-in, your substitute. He did for you what my friend Bobby Aycock did for David. The two were in boot camp in 1959. David was a very likable, yet physically disadvantaged soldier. He had the desire but not the strength. There was simply no way he would pass the fitness test. Too weak for the pull-ups.

But Bobby had such a fondness for David that he came up with a plan. He donned his friend's T-shirt. The shirt bore David's last name, two initials, and service serial number. The superiors didn't know faces; they just read the names and numbers off the shirts and marked scores on a list of names. So Bobby did David's pull-ups. David came out looking pretty good and never even broke a sweat.

Neither did you. Listen, you and I are no match for Satan. Jesus knows this. So he donned our jersey. Better still, he put on our flesh. He was "tempted in every way, just as we are—yet was without sin" (Heb. 4:15 NIV). And because he did, we pass with flying colors.

God gives you Jesus' wilderness grade. Believe that. If you don't, the desert days will give you a one-two punch. The right hook is the struggle. The left jab is the shame for not prevailing against it. Trust his work.

And trust his Word. Don't trust your emotions. Don't trust your opinions. Don't even trust your friends. In the wilderness heed only the voice of God.

Again, Jesus is our model. Remember how Satan teased him? "If you are the Son of God . . ." (Luke 4:3, 9 NCV). Why would Satan say this? Because he knew what Christ had heard at the baptism. "This is My beloved Son, in whom I am well-pleased" (Matt. 3:17).

"Are you really God's Son?" Satan is asking. Then comes the dare— "Prove it!" Prove it by doing something:

"Tell this stone to become bread" (Luke 4:3).

"If You worship before me, it shall all be Yours" (v. 7).

"Throw Yourself down from here" (v. 9).

What subtle seduction! Satan doesn't denounce God; he simply raises doubts about God. Is his work enough? Earthly works—like bread changing or temple jumping—are given equal billing with heavenly works. He attempts to shift, ever so gradually, our source of confidence away from God's promise and toward our performance.

Jesus doesn't bite the bait. No heavenly sign is requested. He doesn't solicit a lightning bolt; he simply quotes the Bible. Three temptations. Three declarations.

"It is written . . ." (v. 4 NCV).

"It is written . . ." (v. 8 NCV).

"It is said . . ." (v. 12).

Jesus' survival weapon of choice is Scripture. If the Bible was enough for his wilderness, shouldn't it be enough for ours? Don't miss the point here. Everything you and I need for desert survival is in the Book. We simply need to heed it.

On a trip to the United Kingdom, our family visited a castle. In the center of the garden sat a maze. Row after row of shoulder-high hedges, leading to one dead end after another. Successfully navigate the labyrinth, and discover the door to a tall tower in the center of the garden. Were you to look at our family pictures of the trip, you'd see four of our five family members standing on the top of the tower. Hmmm, someone is still on the ground. Guess who? I was stuck in the foliage. I just couldn't figure out which way to go.

Ah, but then I heard a voice from above. "Hey, Dad." I looked up to see Sara, peering through the turret at the top. "You're going the wrong way," she explained. "Back up and turn right."

Do you think I trusted her? I didn't have to. I could have trusted my own instincts, consulted other confused tourists, sat and pouted and wondered why God would let this happen to me. But do you know what I did? I listened. Her vantage point was better than mine. She was above the maze. She could see what I couldn't.

Don't you think we should do the same with God? "God is . . . higher than the heavens" (Job 22:12 TLB). "The LORD is high above all nations" (Ps. 113:4). Can he not see what eludes us? Doesn't he want to get us out and bring us home? Then we should do what Jesus did.

Rely on Scripture. Doubt your doubts before you doubt your beliefs. Jesus told Satan, "Man shall not live on bread alone, but on every word that proceeds out of the mouth of God" (Matt. 4:4). The verb *proceeds* is literally "pouring out." Its tense suggests that God is constantly and aggressively communicating with the world through his Word. God is speaking still!

Hang in there. Your time in the desert will pass. Jesus' did. "The devil left Him; and behold, angels came and began to minister to Him" (Matt. 4:11).

Till angels come to you:

Trust his Word. Just like me in the maze, you need a voice to lead you out.

Trust his work. Like David at boot camp, you need a friend to take your place.

Thank God you have One who will.

17

God Gets into Things

Stormy Places
MATTHEW 14:22–33

On a September morning in 2001, Frank Silecchia laced up his boots, pulled on his hat, and headed out the door of his New Jersey house. As a construction worker, he made a living making things. But as a volunteer at the World Trade Center wreckage, he just tried to make sense of it all. He hoped to find a live body. He did not. He found forty-seven dead ones.

Amid the carnage, however, he stumbled upon a symbol—a twenty-foot-tall steel-beam cross. The collapse of Tower One on Building Six created a crude chamber in the clutter. In the chamber, through the dusty sunrise, Frank spotted the cross.

No winch had hoisted it; no cement secured it. The iron beams stood independent of human help. Standing alone, but not alone. Other crosses rested randomly at the base of the large one. Different sizes, different angles, but all crosses.

Several days later engineers realized the beams of the large cross came from two different buildings. When one crashed into another, the two girders bonded into one, forged by the fire.[1]

A symbol in the shards. A cross found in the crisis. "Where is God in all this?" we asked. The discovery dared us to hope, "Right in the middle of it all."

Can the same be said about our tragedies? When the ambulance takes our child or the disease takes our friend, when the economy takes our retirement or the two-timer takes our heart—can we, like Frank, find Christ in the crisis? The presence of troubles doesn't surprise us. The absence of God, however, undoes us.

We can deal with the ambulance if God is in it.

We can stomach the ICU if God is in it.

We can face the empty house if God is in it.

Is he?

Matthew would like to answer that question for you. The walls falling around him were made of water. No roof collapsed, but it seemed as though the sky had.

A storm on the Sea of Galilee was akin to a sumo wrestler's belly flop on a kiddy pool. The northern valley acted like a wind tunnel, compressing and hosing squalls onto the lake. Waves as tall as ten feet were common.

The account begins at nightfall. Jesus is on the mountain in prayer, and the disciples are in the boat in fear. They are "far away from land . . . fighting heavy waves" (Matt. 14:24 NLT). When does Christ come to them? At three o'clock in the morning (v. 25 NLT)! If "evening" began at six o'clock and Christ came at three in the morning, the disciples were alone in the storm for nine hours! Nine tempestuous hours. Long enough for more than one disciple to ask, "Where is Jesus? He knows we are in the boat. For heaven's sake, it was his idea. Is God anywhere near?"

And from within the storm comes an unmistakable voice: "I am."

Wet robe, soaked hair. Waves slapping his waist and rain stinging his face. Jesus speaks to them at once. "Courage! I am! Don't be afraid!" (v. 27).[2]

That wording sounds odd, doesn't it? If you've read the story, you're accustomed to a different shout from Christ. Something like, "Take courage! It is I" (NIV) or "It's all right. . . . I am here!" (NLT) or "Courage, it's me" (MSG).

A literal translation of his announcement results in "Courage! I am! Don't be afraid." Translators tinker with his words for obvious reasons. "I am" sounds truncated. "I am here" or "It is I" feels more complete. But what Jesus shouted in the storm was simply the magisterial: "I am."

The words ring like the cymbal clash in the *1812 Overture.* We've heard them before.

Speaking from a burning bush to a knee-knocking Moses, God announced, "I AM WHO I AM" (Exod. 3:14).

Double-dog daring his enemies to prove him otherwise, Jesus declared, "Before Abraham was born, I am" (John 8:58).

Determined to say it often enough and loud enough to get our attention, Christ chorused:

- "I am the bread of life" (John 6:48).

- "I am the Light of the world" (John 8:12).

- "I am the gate; whoever enters through me will be saved" (John 10:9 NIV).

- "I am the good shepherd" (John 10:11).

- "I am God's Son" (John 10:36 NCV).

- "I am the resurrection and the life" (John 11:25).

- "I am the way, and the truth, and the life" (John 14:6).

- "I am the true vine" (John 15:1).

The present-tense Christ. He never says, "I was." We do. We do because "we were." We were younger, faster, prettier. Prone to be people of the past tense, we reminisce. Not God. Unwavering in strength, he need never say, "I was." Heaven has no rearview mirrors.

Or crystal balls. Our "I am" God never yearns, "Someday I will be."

Again, we do. Dream-fueled, we reach for horizons. "Someday I will . . ." Not God. Can water be wetter? Could wind be windless? Can God be more God? No. He does not change. He is the "I am" God. "Jesus Christ is the same yesterday, today, and forever" (Heb. 13:8 NLT).

From the center of the storm, the unwavering Jesus shouts, "I am." Tall in the Trade Tower wreckage. Bold against the Galilean waves. ICU, battlefield, boardroom, prison cell, or maternity ward—whatever your storm, "I am."

The construction of this passage echoes this point. The narrative is made up of two acts, each six verses long. The first, verses 22–27, centers on the power walk of Jesus. The second, verses 28–33, centers on the faith walk of Peter.

In the first act, Christ comes astride the waves and declares the words engraved on every wise heart: "Courage! I am! Don't be afraid!" In the second act, a desperate disciple takes a step of faith and—for a moment—does what Christ does. He waterwalks. Then he takes his eyes away from Christ and does what we do. He falls.

Two acts. Each with six verses. Each set of six verses contains 90 Greek words. And right in between the two acts, the two sets of verses, and the 180 words is this two-word declaration: "I am."

Matthew, who is good with numbers, reinforces his point. It comes layered like a sub sandwich:

Graphically: Jesus—soaked but strong.

Linguistically: Jesus—the "I am" God.

Mathematically: whether in the words or the weathered world, Jesus—in the midst of it all.

God gets into things! Red Seas. Big fish. Lions' dens and furnaces. Bankrupt businesses and jail cells. Judean wildernesses, weddings, funerals, and Galilean tempests. Look and you'll find what everyone from Moses to Martha discovered. God in the middle of our storms.

That includes yours.

During the days this book was written, a young woman died in our city. She was recently married, the mother of an eighteen-month-old. Her life felt abbreviated. The shelves of help and hope go barren at such times. But at the funeral the officiating priest shared a memory in his eulogy that gave both.

For several years she had lived and worked in New York City. Due to their long friendship, he stayed in constant touch with her via e-mail. Late one night he received a message indicative of God's persistent presence.

She had missed her station on the subway. By the time she realized her mistake, she didn't know what to do. She prayed for safety and some sign of God's presence. This was no hour or place for a young, attractive woman to be passing through a rough neighborhood alone. At that moment the doors opened, and a homeless, disheveled man came on board and plopped down next to her. *God? Are you near?* she prayed. The answer came in a song. The man pulled out a harmonica and played, "Be Thou My Vision"—her mother's favorite hymn.

The song was enough to convince her. Christ was there, in the midst of it all.

Silecchia saw him in the rubble. Matthew saw him in the waves. And you? Look closer. He's there. Right in the middle of it all.

18

Hope or Hype?

The Highest Place
LUKE 9:28–36

Texas State Fair, 1963. A big place and a big night for a wide-eyed eight-year-old boy whose week peaked out at the Dairy Queen on Saturday. The sights and lights of the midway left me quoting Dorothy, "Toto, we're not in Kansas anymore."

The carnival rumbled with excitement. Roller coasters. Ferris wheels. Candied apples, cotton candy, and the Cotton Bowl. And, most of all, the voices.

"Step right up and try your luck!"

"This way, young man. Three shots for a dollar."

"Come on, fellow. Win your mom a teddy bear."

Odysseus and his men never heard sweeter sirens. Do I cut the cards with the lanky fellow at the stand-up booth? Or heed the call of the hefty lady and heave a ball at the dairy bottles? The guy in the top hat and tails dares me to explore the haunted house. "Come in. What's wrong? Afraid?"

A gauntlet of barkers—each taking his turn. Dad had warned me about them. He knew the way of the midway. I can't recall his exact instructions, but I remember the impact. I stuck next to him, my little hand lost in his big one. And every time I heard the voices, I turned to his face. He gave either protection or permission. A roll of the eyes meant "Move on." He smelled a huckster. A smile and a nod said, "Go on—no harm here."

My father helped me handle the voices.

Could you use a little help yourself? When it comes to faith, you likely could. Ever feel as if you are walking through a religious midway?

The Torah sends you to Moses. The Koran sends you to Muhammad. Buddhists invite you to meditate; spiritists, to levitate. A palm reader wants your hand. The TV evangelist wants your money. One neighbor consults her stars. Another reads the cards. The agnostic believes no one can know. The hedonist doesn't care to know. Atheists believe there is nothing to know.

"Step right up. Try my witchcraft."

"Psssst! Over here. Interested in some New Age channels?"

"Hey, you! Ever tried Scientology?"

What do you do? Where's a person to go? Mecca? Salt Lake City? Rome? Therapy? Aromatherapy?

Oh, the voices.

"Father, help me out! Please, modulate one and relegate the others." If that's your prayer, then Luke 9 is your chapter—the day God isolated the authoritative voice of history and declared, "Listen to him."

It's the first scene of the final act in the earthly life of Christ. Jesus has taken three followers on a prayer retreat.

"He took along Peter and John and James, and went up on the mountain to pray. And while He was praying, the appearance of His face became different, and His clothing became white and gleaming" (Luke 9:28–29).

Oh, to have heard that prayer. What words so lifted Christ that his face was altered? Did he see his home? Hear his home?

As a college sophomore, I took a summer job far from home. Too far. My courage melted with each mile I drove. One night I was so homesick I thought my bones would melt. But my parents were traveling, and cell phones were uninvented. Though I knew no one would answer, I called home anyway. Not once or twice, but half a dozen times. The familiar ring of the home phone brought comfort.

Maybe Jesus needed comfort. Knowing that his road home will pass through Calvary, he puts in a call. God is quick to answer. "And behold, two men were talking with Him; and they were Moses and Elijah" (v. 30).

The two were perfect comfort givers. Moses understood tough journeys. Elijah could relate to an unusual exit. So Jesus and Moses and Elijah discuss "His departure which He was about to accomplish at Jerusalem" (v. 31).

Peter, James, and John, meanwhile, take a good nap.

All at once they woke up and saw how glorious Jesus was. They also saw the two men who were with him.

> Moses and Elijah were about to leave, when Peter said to Jesus, "Master, it is good for us to be here! Let us make three shelters, one for you, one for Moses, and one for Elijah." But Peter did not know what he was talking about. (vv. 32–33 CEV)

What would we do without Peter? The guy has no idea what he is saying, but that doesn't keep him from speaking. He has no clue what he is doing but offers to do it anyway. This is his idea: three monuments for the three heroes. Great plan? Not in God's book. Even as Peter is speaking, God starts clearing his throat.

> While he was saying this, a cloud formed and began to overshadow them; and they were afraid as they entered the cloud. Then a voice came out of the cloud, saying, "This is My Son, My Chosen One; listen to Him!" (vv. 34–35)

Peter's error is not that he spoke, but that he spoke heresy. Three monuments would equate Moses and Elijah with Jesus. No one shares the platform with Christ. God comes with the suddenness of a blue norther and leaves Peter gulping. "This is My Son." Not "a son" as if he were clumped in with the rest of us. Not "the best son" as if he were valedictorian of the human race. Jesus is, according to God, "My Son, My Chosen One," absolutely unique and unlike anyone else.[1] So:

"Listen to Him!"

In the synoptic Gospels, God speaks only twice—at the baptism and then here at the Transfiguration. In both cases he begins with "This is My beloved Son." But at the river he concludes with affirmation: "in whom I am well pleased" (Matt. 3:17 NKJV). On the hill he concludes with clarification: "Listen to Him."

He does not command, "Listen to *them.*" He could have. Has a more austere group ever assembled? Moses, the lawgiver. Elijah, the prophet. Peter, the Pentecost preacher. James, the apostle. John, the gospel writer and revelator. The Bible's first and final authors in one place. (Talk about a writers' conference!) God could have said, "These are my priceless servants; listen to them."

But he doesn't. Whereas Moses and Elijah comfort Christ, God crowns

Christ. "Listen to Him . . ." The definitive voice in the universe is Jesus. He is not one among many voices; he is the One Voice over all voices.

You cross a line with that claim. Many people recoil at such a distinction. Call Jesus godly, godlike, God inspired. Call him "a voice" but not "the voice"; a good man but not God-man.

But *good man* is precisely the terminology we cannot use. A good man would not say what he said or claim what he claimed. A liar would. Or a God would. Call him anything in between, and you have a dilemma. No one believed that Jesus was equal with God more than Jesus did.

His followers worshiped him, and he didn't tell them to stop.

Peter and Thomas and Martha called him the Son of God, and he didn't tell them they were wrong.

At his own death trial, his accusers asked, "'Are You the Son of God, then?' And He said to them, 'Yes, I am'" (Luke 22:70).

His purpose, in his words, was to "give his life as a ransom for many" (Matt. 20:28 NIV).

According to Jesus, no one could kill him. Speaking of his life, he said, "I lay it down on My own initiative. I have authority to lay it down, and I have authority to take it up again" (John 10:18).

Could he speak with more aplomb than he did in John 14:9? "He who has seen Me has seen the Father."

And could words be more blasphemous than John 8:58? "Before Abraham was, I AM" (NKJV). The claim infuriated the Jews. "They picked up stones to throw at Him" (v. 59). Why? Because only God is the great I AM. And in calling himself I AM, Christ was equating himself with God. "I am the way, and the truth, and the life; no one comes to the Father but through Me" (John 14:6).

Make no mistake, Jesus saw himself as God. He leaves us with two options. Accept him as God, or reject him as a megalomaniac. There is no third alternative.

Oh, but we try to create one. Suppose I did the same? Suppose you came across me standing on the side of the road. I can go north or south. You ask me which way I'm going. My reply? "I'm going sorth."

Thinking you didn't hear correctly, you ask me to repeat the answer.

"I'm going sorth. I can't choose between north and south, so I'm going both. I'm going sorth."

"You can't do that," you reply. "You have to choose."

"OK," I concede, "I'll head nouth."

"Nouth is not an option!" you insist. "It's either north or south. One way or the other. To the right or to the left. When it comes to this road, you gotta pick."

When it comes to Christ, you've got to do the same. Call him crazy, or crown him as king. Dismiss him as a fraud, or declare him to be God. Walk away from him, or bow before him, but don't play games with him. Don't call him a great man. Don't list him among decent folk. Don't clump him with Moses, Elijah, Buddha, Joseph Smith, Muhammad, or Confucius. He didn't leave that option. He is either God or godless. Heaven sent or hell born. All hope or all hype. But nothing in between.

C. S. Lewis summarized it classically when he wrote:

A man who was merely a man and said the sort of things Jesus said would not be a great moral teacher. He would either be a lunatic—on a level with the man who says he is a poached egg—or else he would be the Devil of Hell. . . . You can shut Him up for a fool, you can spit at Him and kill Him as a demon; or you can fall at His feet and call Him Lord and God. But let us not come with any patronising nonsense about His being a great human teacher. He has not left that open to us. He did not intend to.[2]

Jesus won't be diminished. Besides, do you want him to be? Don't you need a distinctive voice in your noisy world? Of course you do. Don't walk the midway alone. Keep your hand in his and your eyes on him, and when he speaks:

"Listen to him."

19

Abandoned!

Godforsaken Places
MATTHEW 27:45–46

A *bandon.* Such a haunting word.

On the edge of the small town sits a decrepit house. Weeds higher than the porch. Boarded windows and a screen door bouncing with the wind. To the front gate is nailed a sign: *Abandoned.* No one wants the place. Even the poor and desperate pass it by.

A social worker appears at the door of an orphanage. In her big hand is the small, dirty one of a six-year-old girl. As the adults speak, the wide eyes of the child explore the office of the director. She hears the worker whisper, "Abandoned. She was abandoned."

An elderly woman in a convalescent home rocks alone in her room on Christmas. No cards, no calls, no carols.

A young wife discovers romantic e-mails sent by her husband to another woman.

After thirty years on the factory line, a worker finds a termination notice taped to his locker.

Abandoned by family.

Abandoned by a spouse.

Abandoned by big business.

But nothing compares to being abandoned by God.

At noon the whole country was covered with darkness, which lasted for three hours. At about three o'clock Jesus cried out with a loud shout, *"Eli, Eli, lema sabachthani?"* which means, "My God, my God, why did you abandon me?" (Matt. 27:45–46 TEV)

By the time Christ screams these words, he has hung on the cross for six hours. Around nine o'clock that morning, he stumbled to the cleft of Skull Hill. A soldier pressed a knee on his forearm and drove a spike through one hand, then the other, then both feet. As the Romans lifted the cross, they unwittingly placed Christ in the very position in which he came to die—between man and God.

A priest on his own altar.

Noises intermingle on the hill: Pharisees mocking, swords clanging, and dying men groaning. Jesus scarcely speaks. When he does, diamonds sparkle against velvet. He gives his killers grace and his mother a son. He answers the prayer of a thief and asks for a drink from a soldier.

Then, at midday, darkness falls like a curtain. "At noon the whole country was covered with darkness, which lasted for three hours" (v. 45 TEV).

This is a supernatural darkness. Not a casual gathering of clouds or a brief eclipse of the sun. This is a three-hour blanket of blackness. Merchants in Jerusalem light candles. Soldiers ignite torches. Parents worry. People everywhere ask questions. From whence comes this noonday night? As far away as Egypt, the historian Dionysius takes notice of the black sky and writes, "Either the God of nature is suffering, or the machine of the world is tumbling into ruin."[1]

Of course the sky is dark; people are killing the Light of the World.

The universe grieves. God said it would. "On that day . . . I will make the sun go down at noon, and darken the earth in broad daylight. . . . I will make it like the mourning for an only son, and the end of it like a bitter day" (Amos 8:9–10 RSV).

The sky weeps. And a lamb bleats. Remember the time of the scream? "At about three o'clock Jesus cried out." Three o'clock in the afternoon, the hour of the temple sacrifice. Less than a mile to the east, a finely clothed priest leads a lamb to the slaughter, unaware that his work is futile. Heaven is not looking at the lamb of man but at "the Lamb of God, who takes away the sin of the world" (John 1:29 RSV).

A weeping sky. A bleating lamb. But more than anything, a screaming Savior. "Jesus cried out with a loud voice" (Matt. 27:46). Note the sturdy words here. Other writers employed the Greek word for "loud voice" to describe a "roar."[2] Soldiers aren't cupping an ear asking him to speak up. The Lamb roars. "The sun and the moon shall be darkened. . . . The LORD also shall roar out of Zion, and utter his voice from Jerusalem" (Joel 3:15–16 KJV).

Christ lifts his heavy head and eyelids toward the heavens and spends his final energy crying out toward the ducking stars. "*'Eli, Eli, lema sabachthani?'* which means, 'My God, my God, why did you abandon me?'" (Matt. 27:46 TEV).

We would ask the same. Why him? Why forsake your Son? Forsake the murderers. Desert the evildoers. Turn your back on perverts and peddlers of pain. Abandon them, not him. Why would you abandon earth's only sinless soul?

Ah, there is the hardest word. *Abandon.* The house no one wants. The child no one claims. The parent no one remembers. The Savior no one understands. He pierces the darkness with heaven's loneliest question: "My God, my God, why did you abandon me?"

Paul used the same Greek word when he urged Timothy: "Be diligent to come to me quickly; for Demas has *forsaken* me, having loved this present world, and has departed for Thessalonica" (2 Tim. 4:9–10 NKJV, emphasis mine).

As Paul looks for Demas, can he find him? No. Forsaken.

As Jesus looks for God, can he find him? No. Forsaken.

Wait a second. Doesn't David tell us, "I have never seen the righteous forsaken" (Ps. 37:25 NIV)? Did David misspeak? Did Jesus misstep? Neither. In this hour Jesus is anything but righteous. But his mistakes aren't his own. "Christ carried our sins in his body on the cross so we would stop living for sin and start living for what is right" (1 Pet. 2:24 NCV).

Christ carried all our sins in his body . . .

May I get specific for a moment? May I talk about sin? Dare I remind you and me that our past is laced with outbursts of anger, stained with nights of godless passion, and spotted with undiluted greed?

Suppose your past was made public? Suppose you were to stand on a stage while a film of every secret and selfish second was projected on the screen behind you?

Would you not crawl beneath the rug? Would you not scream for the heavens to have mercy? And would you not feel just a fraction . . . just a fraction of what Christ felt on the cross? The icy displeasure of a sin-hating God?

I tasted something similar at the age of sixteen with my own father. He and I were close, best friends. I never feared his abuse or absence. Near the top of my list of blessings is the name Jack Lucado. Near the top of my toughest days is the day I let him down.

Dad had one unbendable rule. No alcohol. He saw liquor dismantle the lives of several of his siblings. If he had his way, it wouldn't touch his family. None was allowed.

Wouldn't you know it? I decided I was smarter than he. A weekend party left me stumbling into the bathroom at midnight and vomiting a belly full of beer. Dad appeared at the door—so angry. He threw a washrag in my direction and walked away.

The next morning I awoke with a headache and the horrible awareness that I had sickened my father's heart. Walking into the kitchen (to this day I could retrace those steps), I saw him seated at the table. His paper was open, but he wasn't reading. Coffee cup was full, but he wasn't drinking. He stared at me, eyes wide with hurt, lips downturned with disbelief. More than any other time in my life, I felt the displeasure of a loving father.

I came undone. How could I survive my father's disgust?

Jesus, enduring a million times more, wondered the same.

Christ carried all our sins in his body . . .

See Christ on the cross? That's a gossiper hanging there. See Jesus? Embezzler. Liar. Bigot. See the crucified carpenter? He's a wife beater. Porn addict and murderer. See Bethlehem's boy? Call him by his other names—Adolf Hitler, Osama bin Laden, and Jeffrey Dahmer.

Hold it, Max. Don't you lump Christ with those evildoers. Don't you place his name in the same sentence with theirs!

I didn't. *He* did. Indeed he did more. More than place his name in the same sentence, he placed himself in their place. And yours.

With hands nailed open, he invited God, "Treat me as you would treat them!" And God did. In an act that broke the heart of the Father, yet honored the holiness of heaven, sin-purging judgment flowed over the sinless Son of the ages.

And heaven gave earth her finest gift. The Lamb of God who took away the sin of the world.

"My God, my God, why did you abandon me?" Why did Christ scream those words?

So you'll never have to.

20

Christ's *Coup de Grâce*

God-Ordained Places

LUKE 22:37

A man and his dog are in the same car. The dog howls bright-moon-in-the-middle-of-the-night caterwauling howls. The man pleads, promising a daily delivery of dog biscuit bouquets if only the hound will hush. After all, it's only a car wash.

Never occurred to him—ahem, to me—that the car wash would scare my dog. But it did. Placing myself in her paws, I can see why. A huge, noisy machine presses toward us, pounding our window with water, banging against the door with brushes. *Duck! We're under attack.*

"Don't panic. The car wash was my idea." "I've done this before." "It's for our own good." Ever tried to explain a car wash to a canine? Dog dictionaries are minus the words *brush* and *detail job.* My words fell on fallen flaps. Nothing helped. She just did what dogs do; she wailed.

Actually, she did what *we* do. Don't we howl? Not at car washes perhaps but at hospital stays and job transfers. Let the economy go south or the kids move north, and we have a wail of a time. And when our Master explains what's happening, we react as if he's speaking Yalunka. We don't understand a word he says.

Is your world wet and wild?

God's greatest blessings often come costumed as disasters. Any doubters need to do nothing more than ascend the hill of Calvary.

Jerusalem's collective opinion that Friday was this: Jesus is finished. What other conclusion made sense? The religious leaders had turned him in. Rome had refused to bail him out. His followers had tucked their tails and scattered. He was nailed to a cross and left to die, which he did. They silenced his lips, sealed his tomb, and, as any priest worth the price of a phylactery would tell you, Jesus is history. Three years of power and promises are decomposing in a borrowed grave. Search the crucifixion sky for one ray of hope, and you won't find it.

Such is the view of the disciples, the opinion of the friends, and the outlook of the enemies. Label it the dog-in-the-passenger-seat view.

The Master who sits behind the wheel thinks differently. God is not surprised. His plan is right on schedule. Even in—*especially* in—death, Christ is still the king, the king over his own crucifixion.

Want proof?

During his final twenty-four hours on earth, what one word did Jesus speak the most? Search these verses for a recurring phrase:

- "I, the Son of Man, must die, as the Scriptures declared long ago" (Matt. 26:24 NLT).

- "Tonight all of you will desert me," Jesus told them. "For the Scriptures say, 'God will strike the Shepherd, and the sheep of the flock will be scattered'" (Matt. 26:31 NLT).

- He could have called thousands of angels to help him but didn't, for this reason. "If I did, how would the Scriptures be fulfilled that describe what must happen now?" (Matt. 26:54 NLT).

- Rather than fault the soldiers who arrested him, he explained that they were players in a drama they didn't write. "But this is all happening to fulfill the words of the prophets as recorded in the Scriptures" (Matt. 26:56 NLT).

- "The Scriptures declare, 'The one who shares my food has turned against me,' and this will soon come true" (John 13:18 NLT).

- To his heavenly Father he prayed: "I guarded them so that not one was lost, except the one headed for destruction, as the Scriptures foretold" (John 17:12 NLT).

- He said to them, "The Scripture says, 'He was treated like a criminal,' and I tell you this scripture must have its full meaning. It was written about me, and it is happening now" (Luke 22:37 NCV).

Did you detect it? *Scripture. Love, sacrifice,* and *devotion* are terms we might expect. But *Scripture* leads the list and reveals this truth: Jesus orchestrated his final days to fulfill Old Testament prophecies. As if he was following a mental list, Jesus checked them off one by one.

Why did Scripture matter to Christ? And why does it matter to us that it mattered to him? Because he loves the Thomases among us. While others kneel and worship, you stroke your chin and wonder if you could see some proof. "How can I know the death of Christ is anything more than the death of a man?"

Begin with the fulfilled prophecy. More Old Testament foretellings were realized during the crucifixion than on any other day. Twenty-nine different prophecies, the youngest of which was five hundred years old, were completed on the day of Christ's death.

What are the odds of such a constellation? The answer staggers the statisticians. Mathematician Peter Stoner estimates the probability of just eight prophecies being fulfilled in one lifetime this way:

Cover the state of Texas two feet deep in silver dollars. On one dollar place one mark. What is the probability that a person could, on the first attempt, select the marked dollar? Those are the same odds that eight prophecies would be satisfied in the life of one man.[1]

But Christ fulfilled twenty-nine in one day! Want some examples?

But He was wounded for our transgressions, He was bruised for our iniquities; the chastisement for our peace was upon Him, and by His stripes we are healed. (Isa. 53:5 NKJV)

They pierced My hands and My feet. (Ps. 22:16 NKJV)

They divide My garments among them,
And for My clothing they cast lots. (Ps. 22:18 NKJV)

"And it shall come to pass in that day," says the Lord GOD, "that I will make the sun go down at noon, and I will darken the earth in broad daylight." (Amos 8:9 NKJV)[2]

Don't call Jesus a victim of circumstances. Call him an orchestrator of circumstances! He engineered the action of his enemies to fulfill prophecy. And he commandeered the tongues of his enemies to declare truth.

Christ rarely spoke on that Friday. He didn't need to. His accusers provided accurate play-by-play. Remember the sign nailed to the cross?

> And Pilate posted a sign over him that read, "Jesus of Nazareth, the King of the Jews." The place where Jesus was crucified was near the city; and the sign was written in Hebrew, Latin, and Greek, so that many people could read it. (John 19:19–20 NLT)

Trilingual truth. Thank you, Pilate, for funding the first advertising campaign of the cross and introducing Jesus as the King of the Jews. And thanks to the Pharisees for the sermon:

> He saved others; himself he cannot save. (Matt. 27:42 KJV)

Could words be more dead-center? Jesus could not, at the same time, save others and save himself. So he saved others.

The award for the most unlikely spokesman goes to the high priest. Caiaphas said, "It is better for one man to die for the people than for the whole nation to be destroyed" (John 11:50 NCV).

Was Caiaphas a believer? Sure sounds like one. Indeed, it *was* better for Christ to die than for all of us to perish. Heaven gets no argument from him. You'd almost think heaven caused him to say what he said. If that's what you think, you are right.

> Caiaphas did not think of this himself. As high priest that year, he was really prophesying that Jesus would die for [the Jewish] nation and for God's scattered children to bring them all together and make them one. (vv. 51–52 NCV)

What's going on here? Caiaphas preaching for Christ? The Pharisees explaining the cross? Pilate painting evangelistic billboards? Out of tragedy emerges triumph. Every disaster proves to be a victory.

This turn of events reminds me of the mule in the well. A mule tumbled down a water shaft. The villagers compared the effort of a rescue with the value of the animal and decided to bury him. They started shoveling dirt. The mule had other ideas. As the clods hit his back, he shook them off and stomped them down. Each spade of earth lifted him higher. He reached the top of the well and walked out. What his would-be killers thought would bury him actually delivered him.

The men who murdered Jesus did the same. Their actions elevated Jesus. Everything—the bad and the good, the evil and the decent— worked together for the *coup de grâce* of Christ.

Should we be surprised? Didn't he promise this would happen? "We know that in everything God works for the good of those who love him" (Rom. 8:28 NCV).

Everything? Everything. Chicken-hearted disciples. A two-timing Judas. A pierced side. Spineless Pharisees. A hardhearted high priest. In every-thing God worked. I dare you to find one element of the cross that he did not manage for good or recycle for symbolism. Give it a go. I think you'll find what I found—every dark detail was actually a golden moment in the cause of Christ.

Can't he do the same for you? Can't he turn your Friday into a Sunday?

Some of you doubt it. How can God use cancer or death or divorce? Simple.

He's smarter than we are. He is to you what I was to four-year-old Amy. I met her at a bookstore. She asked me if I would sign her children's book. When I asked her name, she watched as I began to write, "To Amy . . ."

She stopped me right there. With wide eyes and open mouth, she asked, "How did you know how to spell my name?"

She was awed. You aren't. You know the difference between the knowl-edge of a child and an adult. Can you imagine the difference between the wisdom of a human and the wisdom of God? What is impossible to us is like spelling "Amy" to him. "For as the heavens are higher than the earth, so are My ways higher than your ways and My thoughts than your thoughts" (Isa. 55:9).

I keep taking Molly to the car wash. She's howling less. I don't think she understands the machinery. She's just learning to trust her master.

Maybe we'll learn the same.

21

Christ's Crazy Claim

Incredible Places
MATTHEW 28:1–10

What's the wildest announcement you've ever heard? I'm wondering because I'm about to hear one. Any second now an airlines agent is going to pick up his microphone and . . . wait a minute . . . he's about to talk. I can see him. The guy acts sane. Appears normal. Looks like the kind of fellow who bowls and loves his kids. But what he is about to say qualifies him for a free night in a padded cell. "Ladies and gentlemen, the airplane is now ready. Flight 806 to Chicago will be departing soon. Please listen as we call you to board . . ."

Think about what he just said. He's inviting us to ascend seven miles into the sky in a plane the size of a modern-day ranch house and be hurled through the air at three times the speed of the fastest NASCAR racer in history.

Can you believe what he is asking us to do? Of course you can. But what if you'd never heard such an invitation? Wouldn't you be stunned? Wouldn't you feel like the women who heard this announcement three days after Christ had died on the cross? "He is not here. He has risen from the dead as he said he would" (Matt. 28:6 NCV).

This is what happened:

Early on Sunday morning, as the new day was dawning, Mary Magdalene and the other Mary went out to see the tomb. Suddenly there was a great earthquake, because an angel of the Lord came down from heaven and rolled aside the stone and sat on it. His face shone like lightning, and his clothing was as white as snow. The guards shook with fear when they saw him, and they fell into a dead faint. (Matt. 28:1–4 NLT)

How conditions have changed since Friday. The crucifixion was marked by sudden darkness, silent angels, and mocking soldiers. At the empty tomb the soldiers are silent, an angel speaks, and light erupts like Vesuvius. The one who was dead is said to be alive, and the soldiers, who are alive, look as if they are dead. The women can tell something is up. What they don't know is Someone is up. So the angel informs them: "Don't be afraid! . . . I know you are looking for Jesus, who was crucified. He isn't here! He has been raised from the dead, just as he said would happen. Come, see where his body was lying" (vv. 5–6 NLT).

Such words mess with you. They cause you either to leave the airport or get on the plane. Be they false, the body of Jesus lay like John Brown's, a-moldering in a borrowed grave. Be they false, then we have no good news. An occupied tomb on Sunday takes the good out of Good Friday.

Be they true, however—if the rock is rolled and the Lord is living—then pull out the fiddle and don your dancing shoes. Heaven unplugged the grave's power cord, and you and I have nothing to fear. Death is disabled. Get on board, and let a pilot you've never seen and a power you can't understand take you home.

Can we trust the proclamation? The invitation of the angel is "Come and see . . ."

The empty tomb never resists honest investigation. A lobotomy is not a prerequisite of discipleship. Following Christ demands faith, but not blind faith. "Come and see," the angel invites. Shall we?

Take a look at the vacated tomb. Did you know the opponents of Christ never challenged its vacancy? No Pharisee or Roman soldier ever led a contingent back to the burial site and declared, "The angel was wrong. The body is here. It was all a rumor."

They would have if they could have. Within weeks disciples occupied every Jerusalem street corner, announcing a risen Christ. What quicker way for the enemies of the church to shut them up than to produce a cold and lifeless body? Display the cadaver, and Christianity is stillborn. But they had no cadaver to display.

Helps explain the Jerusalem revival. When the apostles argued for the empty tomb, the people looked to the Pharisees for a rebuttal. But they had none to give. As A. M. Fairbairn put it long ago, "The silence of the Jews is as eloquent as the speech of the Christians!"[1]

Speaking of the Christians, remember the followers' fear at the crucifixion? They ran. Scared as cats in a dog pound. Peter cursed Christ at the fire. Emmaus-bound disciples bemoaned the death of Christ on the trail. After the crucifixion, "the disciples were meeting behind locked doors because they were afraid of the Jewish leaders" (John 20:19 NLT).

These guys were so chicken we could call the Upper Room a henhouse.

But fast-forward forty days. Bankrupt traitors have become a force of life-changing fury. Peter is preaching in the very precinct where Christ was arrested. Followers of Christ defy the enemies of Christ. Whip them and they'll worship. Lock them up and they'll launch a jailhouse ministry. As bold after the Resurrection as they were cowardly before it.

Explanation:

Greed? They made no money.

Power? They gave all the credit to Christ.

Popularity? Most were killed for their beliefs.

Only one explanation remains—a resurrected Christ and his Holy Spirit. The courage of these men and women was forged in the fire of the empty tomb. The disciples did not dream up a resurrection. The Resurrection fired up the disciples. Have doubts about the empty tomb? Come and see the disciples.

While you're searching, come and see the alternatives. If Christ is not raised, if his body is decayed into dust, what are you left with?

How about Eastern mysticism? Let's travel back in time and around the globe to India. It's 490 B.C., and Buddha is willing to see us. Here is our question: "Can you defeat death?" He never opens his eyes, just shakes his head. "You are disillusioned, dear child. Seek enlightenment."

So we do. By virtue of a vigorous imagination, we travel to Greece to meet with the father of logic, Socrates. He offers a sip of hemlock, but we pass, explaining that we have only one question. "Do you have power over the grave? Are you the Son of Zeus?" He scratches his bald head and calls us *raca* (Greek for turkey brains).

Undeterred, we advance a thousand years and locate the ancient village of Mecca. A bearded Muhammad sits in the midst of followers. From the back of the crowd we cry out, "We are looking for Allah incarnate. Are you he?" He stands and rips his robe and demands that we be banished for such heresy.

But we escape. We escape back in time to Jerusalem. We ascend the stairs of a simple house where the King of the Jews is holding court. The room is crowded with earnest disciples. As we find a seat, we look into the radiant face of the resurrected Christ. The love in his eyes is as real as the wounds on his body.

If we ask the question of him—"Are you raised from the dead? Are you the Son of God?"—we know his answer.

Jesus might well personalize the words he gave to the angel. "I am raised from the dead as I said I would be. Come and see the place where my body was."

Quite a claim. Just like passengers in the airport about to board a plane, we get to choose how we respond. Either board and trust the pilot—or try to get home on our own.

I know which choice I prefer.

Conclusion

Still in the Neighborhood

In the aftermath of September 11, 2001, a group of religious leaders was invited by the White House to come to Washington and pray with the president. How my name got on the list, who knows. But I was happy to oblige. Thirty or so of us were seated in a room.

The group was well frocked and well known. Several Catholic cardinals. The president of the Mormon Church and a leader of the B'hai faith. Esteemed Jewish and Muslim spokesmen. Quite ecclesiastically eclectic. Had Christ chosen to return at that moment, a lot of questions would have been answered by who was left standing in the room.

You might wonder if I felt out of place. I lead no denomination. The only time I wear a robe is when I step out of the shower. No one calls me "The Right Most Reverend Lucado." (Although Denalyn promises me she will. Once. Someday. Before I die.)

Did I feel like a minnow in a whale's world? Hardly. I was special among them. And when my turn came to meet George W. Bush, I had to mention why. After giving my name, I added, "And, Mr. President, I was raised in Andrews, Texas." For those of you whose subscription to *National Geographic* has expired, Andrews is only a half-hour drive from Midland, his hometown. Upon learning that we are neighbors, he hitched his britches and smiled that lopsided smile and let his accent drawl ever so slightly. "Why, I know your town. I've walked those streets. I've even played your golf course."

I stood a tad taller. It's nice to know that the most powerful man in the world has walked my streets.

How much nicer to know the same about God.

Yes, he is in heaven. Yes, he rules the universe. But, yes, he has walked your streets. He's still the next door Savior. Near enough to touch. Strong enough to trust. Paul merges these truths into one promise: "Christ Jesus is He who died, yes, rather who was raised, who is at the right hand of God, who also intercedes for us" (Rom. 8:34).

See his divinity? He is "at the right hand of God."

"Right hand of God" equals the highest honor. Is Jesus above all powers? You bet he is:

> He is *far above* any ruler or authority or power or leader or anything else in this world or in the world to come. And God has put all things under the authority of Christ, and he gave him this authority for the benefit of the church. And the church is his body; it is filled by Christ, who fills everything everywhere with his presence. (Eph. 1:21–23 NLT, emphasis mine)

Christ is running the show. Right now. A leaf just fell from a tree in the Alps. Christ caused it to do so. A newborn baby in India inhaled for the first time. Jesus measured the breath. The migration of the belugas through the oceans? Christ dictates their itinerary. He is

> the firstborn of all creation. For by Him all things were created, both in the heavens and on earth, visible and invisible, whether thrones or dominions or rulers or authorities—all things have been created through Him and for Him. (Col. 1:15–16)

What a phenomenal list! Heavens and earth. Visible and invisible. Thrones, dominions, rulers, and authorities. No thing, place, or person omitted. The scale on the sea urchin. The hair on the elephant hide. The hurricane that wrecks the coast, the rain that nourishes the desert, the infant's first heartbeat, the elderly person's final breath—all can be traced back to the hand of Christ, the firstborn of creation.

Firstborn in Paul's vernacular has nothing to do with birth order. *Firstborn* refers to order of rank. As one translation states: "He ranks higher than everything that has been made" (v. 15 NCV). Everything? Find an exception. Peter's mother-in-law has a fever; Jesus rebukes it. A tax needs to be paid; Jesus pays it by sending first a coin and then a fisherman's hook into the mouth of a fish. When five thousand stomachs growl, Jesus renders a boy's basket a bottomless buffet. Jesus exudes authority. He bats an eyelash, and nature jumps. No one argues when, at the end of his earthly life, the God-man declares, "All authority has been given to Me in heaven and on earth" (Matt. 28:18).

> Out of the south comes the storm. . . .
> [God] disperses the cloud of His lightning.
> It changes direction, turning around by His guidance,
> That it may do whatever He commands it
> On the face of the inhabited earth.
> Whether for correction . . .
> Or for lovingkindness, He causes it to happen. . . .
> Stand and consider the wonders of God.
>
> (Job 37:9, 11–14)

Stand and consider, indeed.

- The Hubble Space Telescope sends back infrared images of faint galaxies that are perhaps twelve billion light-years away (twelve billion times six trillion miles).[1]

- Astronomers venture a feeble estimate that the number of stars in the universe equals the number of grains of sand on all the beaches of the world.[2] The star Eta Carinae outshines our sun, in the same way Yankee Stadium outshines a cigarette lighter. Five million times brighter![3]

- The star Betelgeuse has a diameter of 100 million miles, which is larger than the earth's orbit around the sun.[4]

Why the immensity? Why such vast, unmeasured, unexplored, "unused" space? So that you and I, freshly stunned, could be stirred by this resolve: "I can do all things through Christ who strengthens me" (Phil. 4:13 NKJV).

The Christ of the galaxies is the Christ of your Mondays. The Starmaker manages your travel schedule. Relax. You have a friend in high places. Does the child of Arnold Schwarzenegger worry about tight pickle-jar lids? Does the son of Nike founder Phil Knight sweat a broken shoestring? If the daughter of Bill Gates can't turn on her computer, does she panic?

No. Nor should you. The universe's Commander in Chief knows your name. He has walked your streets.

Even in heaven, Christ remains our next door Savior. Even in heaven, he is still "Christ Jesus . . . who died." The King of the universe commands comets with a human tongue and directs celestial traffic with a human hand. Still human. Still divine. Living forever through his two natures. As Peter Lewis states:

> Go to the spiritual heart of this created universe, and you will find a man!
> Go to the place where angels bow who never fell, and you will find a man!
> Go to the very center of the manifested glory of the invisible God, and you will find a man: true human nature, one of our own race, mediating the glory of God![5]

Wait a second, Max. Are you saying that Jesus is still in his fleshly body? That angels worship what Galileans touched? Yes, indeed. Jesus appeared to the followers in a flesh-and-bone body: "A spirit does not have flesh and bones as you see that I have" (Luke 24:39). His resurrected body was a real body, real enough to walk on the road to Emmaus, to be mistaken for that of a gardener, to swallow fish at breakfast.

In the same breath, Jesus' real body was *really* different. The Emmaus disciples didn't recognize him, and walls didn't stop him. Mark tried to describe the new look and settled for "[Jesus] appeared in another form" (Mark 16:12 NKJV). While his body was the same, it was better; it was glorified. It was a heavenly body.

And I can't find the passage that says he shed it. He ascended in it. "He was lifted up while they were looking on, and a cloud received Him out of their sight" (Acts 1:9). He will return in it. The angel told the followers, "This Jesus, who has been taken up from you into heaven, will come in just the same way as you have watched Him go into heaven" (Acts 1:11).

The God-man is still both. The hands that blessed the bread of the boy now bless the prayers of the millions. And the mouth that commissions angels is the mouth that kissed children.

You know what this means? The greatest force in the cosmos understands and intercedes for you. "We have an Advocate with the Father, Jesus Christ the righteous" (1 John 2:1).

Sir John Clarke dedicated many years to Bible translation in the Belgian Congo. He had difficulty translating the word *advocate*. For two years he searched for a suitable translation. His search ended the day he visited the king of the Mulongo people. During the time with the king, an aide appeared, received his instructions, and left. The king told Clarke that the aide was his Nsenga Mukwashi, which was not a name, but a title.

The king explained that the servant represented the people to the king. Clarke immediately asked for permission to watch the man at work. He went to the edge of the village where he found him talking with three women. The husband of one of the women had died, and she was being evicted from her hut. She needed help.

"I will take you to the king," the Nsenga Mukwashi told her.

"Do not do that," she objected. "I am old and timid and would become speechless in his presence."

"There will be no need for you to speak," he assured her. "I shall speak for you."

And he did. Succinctly and clearly and passionately. Clarke noted the flash of anger in the king's eyes. The sovereign ordered his court to care for the widow and seize the culprits. The widow found justice, and Clarke found his word—*Nsenga Mukwashi.*[6]

You, too, have an advocate with the Father. When you are weak, he is strong. When you are timid, he speaks. Your next door Savior is your Nsenga Mukwashi.

> Jesus understands every weakness of ours, because he was tempted in every way that we are. But he did not sin! So whenever we are in need, we should come bravely before the throne of our merciful God. There we will be treated with undeserved kindness, and we will find help. (Heb. 4:15–16 CEV)

Alas, my illustration of the president falls short. Can I call him? Even if I had the number, he's too busy. Yet can I call God? Anytime. He is not too busy for me—or you. Endowed with sleepless attention and endless devotion, he listens. The fact that we can't imagine how he hears a million requests as if they were only one doesn't mean he can't or doesn't. For he can and he does.

And among the requests he hears and heeds is yours. For even though he is in heaven, he never left the neighborhood.

Next Door SAVIOR

DISCUSSION GUIDE

Prepared by Steve Halliday

CHAPTER ONE
OUR NEXT DOOR SAVIOR

TOURING THE NEIGHBORHOOD

1. *Who are you?* he wondered so softly that no one but God could hear. *You just awakened the dead! Should you not be encased in light or encircled by angels or enthroned higher than a thousand Caesars? Yet, look at you—wearing clothes I would wear and laughing at jokes I tell and eating the food we all eat. Is this what death defeaters do? Just who are you?*

   A. When you first learned of Jesus, who did you think he was? Who do you now think he is?

   B. What most amazes you about Jesus? Why?

2. A just-God Jesus could make us but not understand us. A just-man Jesus could love us but never save us. But a God-man Jesus? Near enough to touch. Strong enough to trust. A next door Savior.

   A. What is a "just-God Jesus"? A "just-man Jesus"?

   B. Why would a "just-man Jesus" have no power to save us?

   C. Explain what Max means by a "next door Savior."

3. The cache of Christianity is Christ. Not money in the bank or a car in the garage or a healthy body or a better self-image. . . . Christ is the reward of Christianity.

   A. In what way is Christ the reward of Christianity?

   B. How does our pursuit of Christ affect our everyday actions?

4. Could your world use a little music? If so, invite heaven's baritone to cut loose. He may look as common as the guy next door, but just wait till you see what he can do. Who knows? A few songs with him might change the way you sing. Forever.

   A. In what way could your world use "a little music"?

   B. How could you invite "heaven's baritone to cut loose" in your life?

   C. How does life with Jesus change the way you "sing"?

CITY CENTER

1. Read Luke 7:11–17.

   A. What happened when Jesus saw the funeral procession described in this passage? What did he immediately do (vv. 13–15)?

   B. How did the people react to this incident? What conclusion did they reach (v. 16)?

   C. How did this event demonstrate Jesus' humanity? How did it reveal his divinity?

2. Read Mark 4:35–41.

   A. Why did the storm disturb the disciples' trust?

   B. What reply did Jesus make to the disciples' question (vv. 39–40)?

   C. Given all the disciples had seen Jesus do, why do you think they questioned who Jesus was?

3. Read Colossians 1:15–20; 2:9.

   A. What do these verses teach us about the identity of Jesus? Why is this important?

   B. How do these verses describe a "next door Savior"? What makes him the Savior? In what way is he next door?

COMMUNITY IMPROVEMENT

To help you think of Jesus as your "next door Savior," take a walk through your neighborhood, praying for those who live around you. Ask the Lord to make himself real to them, to show his true nature to them—and ask him how you might help in the process.

CHAPTER TWO
CHRIST'S THEME SONG

TOURING THE NEIGHBORHOOD

1. Why did Jesus hang his family's dirty laundry on the neighborhood clothesline? Because your family has some too.

A. What kind of "dirty laundry" did Jesus mention? Why was it important for him to do so?

B. Based on Jesus' example, what should be our attitude toward our families' past?

2. The phrase "I've been there" is in the chorus of Christ's theme song. To the lonely, Jesus whispers, "I've been there." To the discouraged, Christ nods his head and sighs, "I've been there."

A. Does it help you to know that Christ has experienced the disappointments and hardships of being human? How?

B. In what area of your life is it especially comforting to know that Christ has "been there"? Why?

3. He's not ashamed of you. Nor is he confused by you. Your actions don't bewilder him. Your tilted halo doesn't trouble him. So go to him. After all, you're a part of his family.

A. Do you truly believe Christ is not ashamed of you? How does accepting or rejecting this fact affect your attitude? Your behavior?

B. Do your actions ever bewilder yourself? Explain.

C. In what way are you a part of Christ's family?

D. How do you go to Jesus during times of difficulty? What do you do?

CITY CENTER

1. Read Isaiah 53:2–3.

A. Why do you suppose God chose not to make Christ extraordinary in appearance?

B. What does it mean that Christ grew up as "a root out of parched ground"? What is the "parched ground"? How did this enable him to identify with us?

2. Read Mark 3:20–22.

A. How did Jesus' own family respond to his early ministry (v. 21)? Why do you think they reacted like this?

B. How did the teachers of the law respond to Jesus' teaching (v. 22)? Why do you think they reacted like this?

C. How do you respond to Jesus' teaching? Explain.

3. Read Hebrews 2:10–18.

    A. What does it mean that Jesus was made perfect through sufferings (v. 10)?

    B. Why is Jesus not ashamed to call us his brothers (v. 11)?

    C. Why did the Son of God become human, according to verse 14?

    D. How did Jesus' earthly experience qualify him to become our "high priest" (v. 17)? According to Hebrews 5:1–10, what does Jesus do for us as our high priest?

    E. In what way did Jesus suffer when he was tempted? How did his painful experience benefit us (v. 18)?

COMMUNITY IMPROVEMENT

Jesus went out of his way to identify with us. How do you identify with your neighbors? If you haven't met your next door neighbors yet, determine to do so this week. Invite them over for coffee or out to a movie. Start the process of getting to know them and identifying with their struggles and concerns.

CHAPTER THREE
FRIEND OF FLOPS

TOURING THE NEIGHBORHOOD

1. Jesus starts to smile and shake his head. "Matthew, Matthew, you think I came to quarantine you? Following me doesn't mean forgetting your friends. Just the opposite. I want to meet them."

    A. Why do some people like Matthew think that Jesus came to quarantine them?

    B. Why does Jesus want to meet "flops"—and their friends?

2. What could be better? Sinners and saints in the same room, and no one's trying to determine who is which.

    A. What's good about having saints and sinners in the same room?

    B. What's good about not trying to figure out who belongs to which group?

3. Quite a story. Matthew goes from double-dealer to disciple. He throws a party that makes the religious right uptight, but Christ proud. The good guys look good, and the bad guys hit the road. Some story indeed. What do we do with it?

   A. Why did Matthew's party make the religious right uptight?

   B. What parallel situations do you see today? Do you generally respond to them like Christ or like the religious leaders? Why?

4. You don't have to be weird to follow Jesus. You don't have to stop liking your friends to follow him. Just the opposite. A few introductions would be nice. Do you know how to grill a steak?

   A. Do you know someone who thinks "weirdness" is essential to discipleship?

   B. What are some effective ways you have introduced your friends to Jesus?

   C. What does Max really mean when he asks, "Do you know how to grill a steak?" How would you answer his question?

CITY CENTER

1. Read Matthew 9:9–13.

   A. What problem did the Pharisees have with Jesus' attending Matthew's party (vv. 10–11)? To whom did they direct their question? Why didn't they ask Jesus directly?

   B. Who responded to the Pharisees' question? What reply was given (v. 12)?

   C. Who were the "healthy" in this incident? Who were the "sick"? Did everyone know their true condition? Explain.

   D. What did Jesus tell the Pharisees to go and learn (v. 13)? How could a correct answer begin leading them to spiritual health?

2. Read 1 Corinthians 1:26–31.

   A. What point does Paul make in verse 26? Why is this significant?

   B. How does Paul explain God's actions (vv. 27–29)?

   C. How does Paul describe Jesus' role (v. 30)?

   D. What conclusion does Paul reach (v. 31)?

3. Read Revelation 5:9–10.

   A. How does this song to Jesus describe the people for whom he died? What is their makeup?

   B. What will Jesus do for these people for whom he died? What is their destiny?

COMMUNITY IMPROVEMENT

To become a friend, you have to do more than learn a name; you have to learn a *person*. Be a friend to someone in your area, preferably an older person who could use your help and friendship. Demonstrate your offer of friendship by a creative kindness: Mow a lawn, walk a pet, help with a needed repair, run an errand, or just give your neighbor your phone number, saying "Call me if I can ever help you."

CHAPTER FOUR
THE HAND GOD LOVES TO HOLD

TOURING THE NEIGHBORHOOD

1. Life rushes in. Pale cheeks turn pink. Shallow breaths become full. Hoover Dam cracks and a river floods. The woman feels power enter. And Jesus? Jesus feels power exit.

   A. Try to put yourself in the woman's sandals. How do you think you would have felt at that moment of healing? Surprised? Elated? Astonished? Fearful? Explain.

   B. Why do you think Jesus wanted to know who had touched him? Why was this so important for him, especially since his demand frightened the woman?

2. "The whole story." How long had it been since someone put the gear of life in Park, turned off the key, and listened to her story? But when this woman reaches out to Jesus, he does. With the town bishop waiting, a young girl dying, and a crowd pressing, he still makes time for a woman from the fringe.

   A. Why do you think Jesus wanted to hear the woman's whole story? What did he hope to accomplish?

B. How do you think it benefited the woman to tell her whole story?

C. How does Jesus still make time for "people on the fringe"? How have you personally seen him do this?

3. Illness took her strength. What took yours? Red ink? Hard drink? Late nights in the wrong arms? Long days on the wrong job? Pregnant too soon? Too often? Is her hand your hand? If so, take heart. Your family may shun it. Society may avoid it. But Christ? Christ wants to touch it.

A. Answer Max's question. What took your strength?

B. In what way has this separated you from others? From Christ?

4. Yours is the hand he loves to hold.

A. Do you believe this statement? Explain.

B. How does Jesus "hold" our hands today? In what instances of your life has he held your hand?

City Center

1. Read Mark 5:21–34.

A. What request did the synagogue ruler make of Jesus (v. 23)? How did Jesus respond (v. 24)?

B. Describe the woman's problem (vv. 25–26). What would be comparable today to her situation?

C. How was her touch different from the touch of all the others around Jesus? How did the disciples react to his question about who touched him (v. 31)?

D. How did Jesus respond to the woman's confession (v. 34)?

2. Read Mark 10:13–16.

A. Why did the disciples rebuke certain people? To what did the disciples object (v. 13)?

B. How did Jesus react to the disciples' action (v. 14)? What reason did he give for his reaction (vv. 14–15)?

C. What did Jesus do to emphasize his point (v. 16)?

3. Read Isaiah 42:1, 5–7.

   A. Who is speaking in this passage? How does the prophet describe him (v. 5)?

   B. What does God promise to do for his "Servant" (v. 6)? To whom is he sending this Servant?

   C. How does the touch of God affect the Servant, and then how does the touch of the Servant affect us (v. 7)?

COMMUNITY IMPROVEMENT

It has been said that the hands of his disciples are the hands of Christ to the world. As his follower, you can "touch" the people in your world for him. Do a little research to see where a "helping hand" might be needed in your own neighborhood or community. Can you volunteer at a food bank, serve as a story reader at a local grade school, offer to serve a meal at a homeless shelter? Find out what the opportunities are, and then take advantage of one. Be the hands of Christ.

CHAPTER FIVE
TRY AGAIN

TOURING THE NEIGHBORHOOD

1. There is a look that says, "It's too late."

   A. What kind of look says, "It's too late"? Have you seen this look? Explain.

   B. Have you ever worn this kind of look? Explain.

2. You've felt what Peter felt. You've sat where Peter sat. And now Jesus is asking you to go fishing. He knows your nets are empty. He knows your heart is weary. He knows you'd like nothing more than to turn your back on the mess and call it a life. But he urges, "It's not too late to try again."

   A. What is making you feel weary right now?

   B. In what way might Jesus be asking you to "go fishing"?

3. Spotting treasures is easy for the one who hid them. Finding fish is simple for the God who made them. To Jesus, the Sea of Galilee is a dollar-store fishbowl on a kitchen cabinet.

   A. If Jesus could so easily find hard-to-find fish on the Sea of Galilee, what kind of hard-to-find "fish" would you like him to point out in your own sea?

   B. How would your life change if you consciously remembered all of the time that Jesus was (and is) God in the flesh?

4. Contrary to what you may have been told, Jesus doesn't limit his recruiting to the stout-hearted. The beat up and worn out are prime prospects in his book, and he's been known to climb into boats, bars, and brothels to tell them, "It's not too late to start over."

   A. In what ways do we sometimes think that Jesus *does* limit his recruiting to the stout-hearted? Why do we believe this myth?

   B. Who have you known that started over? How far did Jesus go to reach them? How did they respond?

   C. Has Jesus ever told you, "It's not too late to start over"? Explain.

CITY CENTER

1. Read Luke 5:1–11.

   A. What request did Jesus make of Simon Peter in verse 3? Why did he make the request?

   B. What request did Jesus make of Simon in verse 4?

   C. How did Simon respond to Jesus' request (v. 5)? What did he do anyway?

   D. What happened when Simon complied with Jesus' request (vv. 6–7)?

   E. Why did Simon respond as he did to the miracle (vv. 8–10)?

   F. How did Jesus respond to Simon's reaction (v. 10)?

   G. Why do you think Simon and his partners left everything to follow Jesus?

2. Read Romans 7:14–25.

   A. How does Paul characterize himself in verse 14? Why is this significant?

   B. What personal problem does Paul describe in verses 15–23? Can you identify with this problem? Explain.

   C. How does this problem make the apostle feel (v. 24)? Can you identify with this? Explain.

   D. What question does Paul ask in verse 24? What answer does he give in verse 25? What does all this have to do with "trying again"?

COMMUNITY IMPROVEMENT

Most of us have a neighbor or friend or family member with whom we've had a disagreement or conflict. Perhaps you've already tried, unsuccessfully, to mend fences. Why not try again? What's keeping you from making another attempt? Before you approach this person, commit to spending at least an hour in prayer about your attitude, your fears, and your goal. Then . . . try again!

CHAPTER SIX
SPIT THERAPY

TOURING THE NEIGHBORHOOD

1. Talk about a thankless role. Selected to suffer. Some sing to God's glory. Others teach to God's glory. Who wants to be blind for God's glory? Which is tougher—the condition or discovering it was God's idea?

   A. Would you like to sing for God's glory? Teach to God's glory? Be blind for God's glory? Explain.

   B. Which do you think would be tougher, to be blind or to learn your condition was God's idea? Explain.

   C. How would you explain this story to someone outside the faith? How would you explain that God allowed someone to be born blind—and live in that condition for many years—so others could see his glory when he healed him?

2. Who was really blind that day? The neighbors didn't see the man; they saw a novelty. The church leaders didn't see the man; they saw a technicality. The parents didn't see their son; they saw a social difficulty. In the end, no one saw him.

   A. What people in our culture does no one "see"?

   B. Have you ever felt invisible to others? Explain.

   C. What examples can you think of where we daily overlook the miracles occurring around us and perhaps instead focus on the negative?

3. Do some people seem to be dealt more than their share of bad hands? If so, Jesus knows. He knows how they feel, and he knows where they are.

   A. Answer Max's question.

   B. Who in your life seems to have been dealt more than his or her share of bad hands? Describe the person's situation. How have you seen people respond differently to great difficulties? What was the result in each case?

   C. Why do you think God allows this uneven sharing of life's hands?

4. I'm sorry about your greasy gown. And your flowers—they tend to slide, don't they? Who has an answer for the diseases, drudgeries, and darkness of this life? I don't. But we do know this. Everything changes when you look at your groom.

   A. How do you respond to the diseases, drudgeries, and darkness of this life?

   B. What changes when you look at your groom?

CITY CENTER

1. Read John 9:1–41.

   A. What question began this whole incident (v. 2)? How are some forms of this question still being asked today?

   B. How did the man's neighbors react to his healing (vv. 8–10)? Why do you think they responded like this?

    C. How did the Pharisees react to the man's healing (vv. 13–16)? Why did they react like this?

    D. How did the man's parents react to their son's healing (vv. 18–23)? Why did they react like this?

    E. In what way did the man show courage the second time the religious leaders summoned him (vv. 24–33)? How did the leaders react to his courage (v. 34)?

    F. How did Jesus react to the ill treatment of the man (vv. 35–37)? How did the man react to Jesus, once he heard the truth (v. 38)?

2. Read 2 Corinthians 4:16–18.

    A. How can we keep from losing heart, according to verse 16?

    B. How does verse 17 help us to keep moving ahead spiritually, despite unexplained suffering?

    C. What strategy for living does verse 18 develop? How do you fix your eyes on the unseen? What are some practical ways to do this?

COMMUNITY IMPROVEMENT

Who in your life needs a little encouragement right now? What can you do to brighten an otherwise gloomy day? Don't let another day go by without doing what you can to bring some cheer into that person's life, whether through a phone call, a thoughtfully written letter, a personal visit, or something else more appropriate.

CHAPTER SEVEN
WHAT JESUS SAYS AT FUNERALS

TOURING THE NEIGHBORHOOD

1. Every funeral has its Marthas. Sprinkled among the bereaved are the bewildered. "Help me understand this one, Jesus."

    A. Have you ever been a "Martha" at a funeral? If so, describe how you felt.

    B. Whose death has most bewildered you? Why?

2. Jesus weeps. He weeps with them. He weeps for them. He weeps with you. He weeps for you.

   A. How does it make you feel to know that Jesus weeps over human tragedy?

   B. What does it mean that Jesus weeps "with" us?

   C. What does it mean that Jesus weeps "for" us?

3. Grief does not mean you don't trust; it simply means you can't stand the thought of another day without the Jacob or Lazarus of your life.

   A. Why do we sometimes think that grieving *does* mean we're not trusting?

   B. Does there come a point where grieving crosses over into a failure to trust? Explain.

4. When Christ speaks to the dead, the dead listen. Indeed, had Jesus not addressed Lazarus by name, the tenant of every tomb on earth would have stepped forth.

   A. Do you agree with Max's statements? What does this say about Christ's power over the dead? Over the living?

   B. Is there someone you have given up on, thinking he or she would never "hear" Christ's voice? How does this encourage you?

CITY CENTER

1. Read John 11:1–44.

   A. Why does verse 4 seem to contradict verse 14? In what way was the contradiction resolved?

   B. Why did Jesus stay where he was for three days before going to see his friend Lazarus? What was Jesus' priority?

   C. Why do you think Jesus did not tell the sisters what he was about to do? Why did he keep it a secret until he did it?

   D. How did the sisters show both trust and doubt in this story? How do we often do the same?

2. Read Romans 14:8–10.

   A. What kinds of people belong to the Lord, according to verse 8? Why is this significant?

   B. Why did Christ die and rise again, according to verse 9?

   C. How does Paul apply this theological truth to a very practical problem in verse 10?

3. Read 1 Thessalonians 4:13–18.

   A. What prompted Paul to write this passage, according to verse 13?

   B. How did Paul intend to encourage his friends who had lost believing loved ones (vv. 14–17)?

   C. What did Paul want his friends to do with the instruction he gave them (v. 18)? Why did he make this request?

COMMUNITY IMPROVEMENT

Read a compassionate and well-written work on grief or caring for the grieving, such as C. S. Lewis's *A Grief Observed* or Charles Swindoll's *For Those Who Hurt.* Make it a goal to learn something new about how you can help in the grieving process, and then look for ways to put your new knowledge to work.

CHAPTER EIGHT
GETTING THE HELL OUT

TOURING THE NEIGHBORHOOD

1. Satan does not sit still. A glimpse of the wild man reveals Satan's goal for you and me. *Self-imposed pain.* The demoniac used rocks. We are more sophisticated; we use drugs, sex, work, violence, and food. (Hell makes us hurt ourselves.)

   A. How have you seen people around you suffer from self-imposed pain?

   B. In what way(s) has hell made you hurt yourself?

   C. How did you deal with this self-imposed pain?

2. Satan can disturb us, but he cannot defeat us. The head of the serpent is crushed.

   A. What does it mean that Satan cannot "defeat" us?

   B. What does it mean that the head of the serpent is crushed?

   C. How is Satan disturbing you or your family at this moment?

3. One word from Christ, and the demons are swimming with the swine, and the wild man is "clothed and in his right mind." Just one command! No séance needed. No hocus-pocus. No chants were heard or candles lit. Hell is an anthill against heaven's steamroller.

   A. Why could Christ control the demons with a single command?

   B. What does it mean for you that Christ has such power over hell?

4. The snake in the ditch and Lucifer in the pit—both have met their match. And, yet, both stir up dust long after their defeat. For that reason, though confident, we are still *careful*. For a toothless ol' varmint, Satan sure has some bite!

   A. How are you "careful" in dealing with Satan and his forces?

   B. Describe some recent examples of Satan's "bite."

City Center

1. Read Mark 5:1–20.

   A. Why do you think the demon-possessed man came out to meet Jesus when the Lord got out of the boat (v. 2)? Why wouldn't he just run away?

   B. What request did the man make of Jesus (v. 7)? Why do you think he made this request?

   C. Why do you think the demons wanted to enter the pigs (v. 12)?

   D. How did the townspeople respond to this divine show of force (vv. 14–17)?

   E. What did the cured man request of Jesus (v. 18)? What answer did Jesus give (v. 19)? Why do you think he gave this answer?

2. Read 1 Peter 5:8–10.

    A. How does this passage picture the devil (v. 8)? Why is this an apt description?

    B. How are you to "resist" Satan (v. 9)?

    C. How do you steady yourself so that you stand "firm in your faith"?

    D. Why does it help to remember that you are not alone in suffering and temptation (v. 9)?

    E. From where does all spiritual strength ultimately come (v. 10)?

3. Read Ephesians 6:10–18.

    A. Why does a Christian need spiritual armor and spiritual weapons (vv. 11–12)?

    B. What sort of armor does Paul describe here? What sort of weaponry?

    C. Name each of the items listed here. Which ones do you think you have a good grip on? Which ones need more of your attention? Why?

COMMUNITY IMPROVEMENT

The topic of spiritual warfare can scare off a lot of people and bring out the kookiness in others, but Scripture makes it clear that we are in a very real spiritual battle. Read 2 Corinthians 10:3–5, and make a list of what you need to improve in this area. Share your list with a trusted friend, and ask him or her to keep you accountable to work on it.

CHAPTER NINE
IT'S NOT UP TO YOU

TOURING THE NEIGHBORHOOD

1. God doesn't send us to obedience school to learn new habits; he sends us to the hospital to be given a new heart. Forget training; he gives transplants.

    A. Why do we need new hearts rather than mere obedience?

    B. Do you have a new heart? Explain.

    C. What are the indications of a new heart? How do they contrast with acts of mere obedience?

2. There is no Rewind button on the VCR of life . . . is there? We don't get to start over . . . do we? A man can't be born again . . . can he?

   A. Have you ever wanted to hit the Rewind button on the VCR of life? What would you like to go back and change? Since you can't change the past, how could you use it for good?

   B. How does God allow us to "start over"? What does this look like?

   C. What does it mean to you to be "born again"?

3. The stumbles of a toddler do not invalidate the act of birth. And the stumbles of a Christian do not annul his spiritual birth.

   A. Why do we sometimes think that stumbles invalidate spiritual birth?

   B. How do you feel when you stumble? Does it bother you? Explain.

   C. What kind of stumbles are you most prone to take?

4. He has deposited a Christ seed in you. As it grows, you will change. It's not that sin has no more presence in your life, but rather that sin has no power over your life. Temptation will pester you, but temptation will not master you.

   A. What is the "Christ seed" that God deposits in his children?

   B. How have you changed since you first became a Christian?

   C. Does temptation have a tendency more often to pester or master you? Explain.

CITY CENTER

1. Read John 3:1–16.

   A. Why do you think Nicodemus came to see Jesus at night?

   B. Name some similarities and differences between physical and spiritual birth.

   C. Who takes the lead role in spiritual birth (v. 8)? Why is this important?

   D. What role does belief or trust play in spiritual birth (v. 15)?

   E. What is promised to those who place their trust in Christ (v. 16)?

2. Read Titus 3:3–6.

   A. How does Paul characterize his life and that of his friends before their conversion (v. 3)?

   B. Who took the lead role in their conversions (vv. 4–5)?

   C. How does Paul picture his salvation (v. 5)?

   D. What part did Jesus Christ play in this accomplishment (v. 6)?

3. Read Philippians 1:3–6.

   A. Why does Paul say he prays for the Philippians (vv. 3–5)?

   B. Who "began a good work" in Paul's friends (v. 6)? What does this mean?

   C. Who will bring to completion this work in Paul's friends? How will he do this?

COMMUNITY IMPROVEMENT

Believers who stumble in their walk of faith often feel like failures and sometimes wonder whether God can even stand them anymore. Think of someone you know who has taken a nasty stumble in the past few days or weeks. What could you do to help this person recover from the fall and get on with life in Christ? Make a plan and then put it into action.

CHAPTER TEN
THE TRASHMAN

TOURING THE NEIGHBORHOOD

1. His voice is warm and his question honest. "Will you give me your trash?"

   A. What is the "trash" mentioned here?

   B. What sort of "trash" do you carry around?

   C. Do you tend to hand over or hang on to your trash? Explain.

2. By the time they reach the hill, the line to the top is long. Hundreds walk ahead of them. All wait in silence, stunned by what they hear—a scream, a pain-pierced roar that hangs in the air for moments, interrupted only by a groan. Then the scream again. His.

    A. Why did the Trashman scream?

    B. Why did the Trashman subject himself to such pain?

3. Her words are soft, intended for no one. "He's standing." Then aloud, for her friend, "He's standing." And louder for all, "He's standing!" She turns; all turn. They see him silhouetted against a golden sun. Standing. Indeed.

    A. What does this image of the Trashman standing represent in our world?

    B. How does it make you feel to know that a risen Christ is standing?

CITY CENTER

1. Read John 1:29–31.

    A. Why did John the Baptist call Jesus "the Lamb of God"?

    B. Given their culture, how would John's audience have interpreted the reference to a lamb?

    C. Since Jesus was born several months after John, in what way was Jesus "before" John (v. 30)?

    D. Using a Bible concordance, look up several different types of references to "lambs." In what ways was Jesus like a lamb?

2. Read 2 Corinthians 5:17–6:2.

    A. How does being a "new creature" in Christ relate to the picture of laying one's trash before the Trashman?

    B. When God redeems us (and takes away our trash), what does he ask us to do in return (vv. 18–20)?

    C. When is the best time to give God your trash (v. 2)?

COMMUNITY IMPROVEMENT

What "trash" do you tend to carry around with you? How is it weighing you down? What keeps you from placing this garbage at the feet of Jesus? Set aside a good chunk of time today, and bring all of this trash to your Savior. Spend at least a half-hour in prayer, confessing whatever you need to confess and asking the Lord to carry your burden for you. Make sure to close your prayer time with healthy praise for the One who offers to carry your burdens.

CHAPTER ELEVEN
HE LOVES TO BE WITH THE ONES HE LOVES

TOURING THE NEIGHBORHOOD

1. Holiday travel. It isn't easy. Then why do we do it? Why cram the trunks and endure the airports? You know the answer. We love to be with the ones we love.

   A. Describe the last time you took a holiday trip. What challenges did it present?

   B. If we love to be with the ones we love, then why are we so often separated from them?

2. What a world he left. Our classiest mansion would be a tree trunk to him. Earth's finest cuisine would be walnuts on heaven's table.

   A. What, to you, is the most remarkable thing about Jesus' leaving heaven to come to earth?

   B. Why do you think Jesus left heaven to live among us on earth?

3. Speaking through the door, Dr. Maltz told the man of his wife's proposal. "She wants me to disfigure her face, to make her face like yours in the hope that you will let her back into your life. That's how much she loves you." There was a brief moment of silence, and then, ever so slowly, the doorknob began to turn.

   A. What finally got through to the man? What force drove him to change his mind?

   B. Have you ever experienced human love as great as that of the wife in the story? Explain.

4. God took on our face, our disfigurement. He became like us. Just look at the places he was willing to go: feed troughs, carpentry shops, badlands, and cemeteries. The places he went to reach us show how far he will go to touch us.

A. How did Jesus take on our disfigurement? Why did he do so?

B. What nasty places have you seen Jesus go to? What did he do there?

C. Where did Jesus find you? Describe what happened.

CITY CENTER

1. Read Philippians 2:4–11.

   A. What command are we given in verse 4? What's hard and what's easy about following this command?

   B. What kind of example did Jesus set for us? Name some specific areas.

   C. How will God reward Jesus for his obedience (vv. 9–11)? How is this meant to encourage us?

2. Read John 1:14.

   A. Who is "the Word" in this verse? How do you know?

   B. From where did this Word come?

   C. What does it mean that he was "full" of truth?

   D. What does it mean that he was "full" of grace?

3. Read John 14:15–18.

   A. How do we prove our love for Jesus, according to verse 15?

   B. To whom will Jesus send another "Helper" or "Counselor" or "Comforter," according to verse 16? Who is this Helper?

   C. Where can we find this Helper (v. 17)?

   D. What promise did Jesus make in verse 18? How is he keeping it today? How does this show that he loves to be with the ones he loves?

COMMUNITY IMPROVEMENT

The book of Hebrews talks about sympathizing with those in prison (10:34) and remembering them as if we were there with them (13:3). Have you ever considered visiting someone in prison? Do a little research to see what local ministries reach out to prisoners, or check out www.pfm.org (Prison Fellowship's Web site) to get some helpful direction. And then plan a trip!

CHAPTER TWELVE
WHAT'S IT LIKE?

TOURING THE NEIGHBORHOOD

1. The first stop on Christ's itinerary was a womb. Where will God go to touch the world? Look deep within Mary for an answer.

    A. Why do you think God bothered with a human birth? If he did an "end around" a human father, why not do another "end around" a human mother?

    B. What is most remarkable to you about Mary? According to human wisdom, why might she seem an unlikely choice?

2. Christ grew in Mary until he had to come out. Christ will grow in you until the same occurs. He will come out in your speech, in your actions, in your decisions. Every place you live will be a Bethlehem, and every day you live will be a Christmas.

    A. How is Christ coming out in your speech, your actions, your decisions?

    B. Can you say that everywhere you live is a Bethlehem? Explain.

3. You are a modern-day Mary. Even more so. He was a fetus in her, but he is a force in you. He will do what you cannot.

    A. Do you have trouble thinking of yourself as a "modern-day Mary"? Explain.

    B. Describe some things that Jesus has done through you that you couldn't have done on your own.

4. If Mary is our measure, God seems less interested in talent and more interested in trust.

    A. Why would God be more interested in trust than in talent?

    B. Is this good news for you or bad? Explain.

CITY CENTER

1. Read Luke 1:26–38.

    A. How did the angel greet Mary (v. 28)? How did Mary react (v. 29)? Why?

B. What promise did the angel give to Mary (vv. 30–33)? What important details did he seem to leave out (v. 34)?

C. How did the angel answer Mary's lone question (v. 35)? In what way did this answer really not give many answers?

D. How did Mary respond to the whole announcement (v. 38)? What does this show about her?

2. Read Acts 26:9–24.

A. How did Paul describe himself before he met Jesus on the road to Damascus (vv. 9–11)?

B. According to 2 Corinthians 6:4–10, how did Paul describe his life after he met Jesus?

C. According to Galatians 2:20, to what did Paul attribute the remarkable change in his life?

3. Read Ephesians 3:16–19.

A. What prayer did Paul offer for the Ephesians in verse 16? Name the various elements of this prayer.

B. What does it mean for Christ to "dwell" in a person's heart "through faith"?

C. What further prayer did Paul offer in verse 18? How does this prayer build upon his previous one?

D. What did Paul see as the final answer of this prayer (v. 19)?

COMMUNITY IMPROVEMENT

What are you currently doing in your Christian life that you absolutely could *not* do if Christ were not working through you? Make a list of these things. If your list seems short, make a one-month commitment to God to pray for his instruction and leading in this area. Ask God to show you how to let Christ live through you in everyday, "normal" kinds of activities—and then note what changes start to come.

CHAPTER THIRTEEN
A Cure for the Common Life

Touring the Neighborhood

1. You lead a common life. Punctuated by occasional weddings, job transfers, bowling trophies, and graduations—a few highlights— but mainly the day-to-day rhythm that you share with the majority of humanity.

   A. What is "common" about your life?

   B. What is extraordinary about your life?

2. For thirty of his thirty-three years, Jesus lived a common life. Aside from that one incident in the temple at the age of twelve, we have no record of what he said or did for the first thirty years he walked on this earth.

   A. Why do you think Jesus waited until about the age of thirty to begin his public ministry?

   B. What value was there in Jesus' thirty years of "common life"?

3. Next time your life feels ordinary, take your cue from Christ. Pay attention to your work and your world.

   A. Do you like feeling "ordinary"? Explain.

   B. How could you make "ordinary" experiences extraordinary?

4. What kind of love adopts disaster? What kind of love looks into the face of children, knowing full well the weight of their calamity, and says, "I'll take them"?

   A. Answer these questions.

   B. Why would God say these things about us? Why would he adopt us?

City Center

1. Read Mark 6:1–6.

   A. Why did the preaching of Jesus astonish his hometown neighbors (vv. 2–3)?

B. How did Jesus respond to the comments of his neighbors (vv. 4–6)?

C. Why was Jesus amazed at his neighbors?

2. Read 1 Peter 1:17–21.

A. What does it mean to live in "reverent fear" (v. 17 NIV)? What does this look like?

B. How does Peter describe the kind of life handed down to us (v. 18)?

C. How does Peter describe the one who redeemed us (v. 19)?

D. What are the human and divine elements in Jesus' life described in verse 20?

E. In whom do we place our faith, according to verse 21? Through whom do we exercise this faith? What is significant about this?

COMMUNITY IMPROVEMENT

Some Christians get off on an unhealthy track because they desperately want to be seen as anything but ordinary. But read 1 Thessalonians 4:11–12. What does Paul say here about an ordinary Christian life? To what does it lead? What might you have to do, if anything, to get more in step with this instruction? Commit these two verses to memory, and meditate on them for the next week or two. Look for an unheralded, "ordinary" opportunity to serve.

CHAPTER FOURTEEN
OH, TO BE DTP-FREE!

TOURING THE NEIGHBORHOOD

1. Do you have any DTPs? When you see the successful, are you jealous? When you see the struggler, are you pompous? If someone gets on your bad side, is that person as likely to get on your good side as I am to win the Tour-de-France?

A. Describe what Max means by a Destructive Thought Pattern (DTP).

B. Answer his questions. What other DTPs come to mind?

2. Lust wooed him. Greed lured him. Power called him. Jesus—the human—was tempted. But Jesus—the holy God—resisted. Contaminated e-mail came his way, but he resisted the urge to open it.

   A. How could a sinless Son of God actually be tempted? What would it mean for us if he couldn't be tempted?

   B. How did Jesus resist the urge to open the "contaminated e-mail"? How can we do the same?

3. Remember the twelve-year-old boy in the temple? The one with sterling thoughts and a Teflon mind? Guess what. That is God's goal for you! You are made to be like Christ!

   A. In what ways do you wish you were more like Christ? Be specific.

   B. Describe someone whose faith you respect. In what ways does this person model Christ to you?

4. He changes the man by changing the mind. And how does it happen? By doing what you are doing right now. Considering the glory of Christ.

   A. What does it mean to consider "the glory of Christ"?

   B. How often do you let your mind ponder the person and work of Jesus? What is most effective in helping you to do this?

CITY CENTER

1. Read Luke 2:41–50.

   A. Why do you think Jesus neglected to tell his parents that he was going to stay behind in Jerusalem?

   B. What sort of questions do you imagine Jesus asked the teachers in the temple?

   C. Why do you think Jesus asked his parents the questions he raised in verse 49?

   D. Why do you think Jesus' parents did not understand what he said to them?

   E. Luke tells us that Jesus was obedient to his parents, even though they misunderstood him (v. 50). How is this significant?

2. Read Romans 8:5–11.

   A. What test does Paul give in verse 5 for telling whether we are pursuing God or our own selfish interests?

   B. What does the sinful mind produce (v. 6)? What does the godly mind produce?

   C. How can we make sure that our minds experience peace and life (v. 9)? What does this require, practically speaking?

   D. What promise are we given in verse 11?

3. Read Colossians 3:1–17.

   A. What instruction does Paul give us in verses 1–2? What does this mean in practical terms?

   B. How does Paul "flesh out" his command in the verses that follow? How can you tell if you are complying with his instructions or not?

   C. Create a two-column list. On the right side, put the "good" qualities Paul says we are to pursue; on the left, put the "bad" qualities we are to avoid. How does striving for the mind of Christ lead naturally to this way of life?

COMMUNITY IMPROVEMENT

Up for a challenge? It's not an "easy" book, but John Piper's *Future Grace* has some terrific guidance and insights into conquering specific temptations that everyone faces. He demonstrates how to use particular Scripture verses to combat several besetting sins, such as anxiety, pride, shame, impatience, bitterness, lust, and despondency. Get a copy of the book and start reading the section on the temptation that causes you the most trouble.

CHAPTER FIFTEEN
TIRE KICKER TO CAR BUYER

TOURING THE NEIGHBORHOOD

1. Baptism wasn't a new practice. It was a required rite for any Gentile seeking to become a Jew. Baptism was for the moldy, second-class,

unchosen people, not the clean, top-of-the-line class favorites—the Jews. Herein lies the rub. John refuses to delineate between Jew and Gentile. In his book, every heart needs a detail job.

A. Why did John believe that "every heart needs a detail job"?

B. In what way does *your* heart need a detail job? Explain.

2. What do we owe? We owe God a perfect life. Perfect obedience to every command.

A. Do you agree with these statements? Why or why not?

B. If you stopped at the requirement, how would you feel? Why?

3. Baptism celebrates your decision to take a seat. . . . We are not saved by the act, but the act demonstrates the way we are saved. We are given credit for a perfect life we did not lead—indeed, a life we could never lead.

A. How does the act of baptism celebrate and demonstrate the way we are saved?

B. Why do you think God uses physical acts to serve as spiritual markers?

4. The daughter answered the doorbell that evening to find a seven-foot-tall, brightly wrapped box. She tore it open, and out stepped her father, fresh off the plane from the West Coast. Can you imagine her surprise? Perhaps you can. Your gift came in the flesh too.

A. How did your Father become a gift?

B. What have you done with this gift? What are you doing with this gift?

CITY CENTER

1. Read Matthew 3:13–17.

A. Why do you think Jesus wanted to be baptized by John?

B. How did John react to Jesus' wish to be baptized (v. 14)?

C. In what way did Jesus' baptism "fulfill all righteousness" (v. 15)?

D. How did God demonstrate his approval of Jesus at this event (vv. 16–17)?

2. Read Romans 6:3–7.

   A. What does Paul mean that Christians are "baptized" into the death of Christ (v. 3)?

   B. How does baptism symbolize the beginning of a new way of life (v. 4)?

   C. If we are "buried" with Christ in baptism, to what are we "raised" (v. 5)?

3. Read Galatians 3:26–29.

   A. How does one become a son of God, according to verse 26?

   B. What does it mean to be "clothed with Christ" (v. 27)?

   C. How does this "clothing" lead to Paul's statement in verse 28?

   D. What promise does Paul reiterate in verse 29?

COMMUNITY IMPROVEMENT

Have you followed the Lord in baptism? If you have made a commitment of faith to Christ, why not? If this is a step of obedience which you're ready to take, then get it on the schedule. Make an appointment with your pastor to talk about what's involved in baptism and what it means, and then prepare yourself for the event. Invite family and friends—hey, why not neighbors too?—and make it the celebration God means it to be. If you already have been baptized, find out when a friend or loved one is scheduled to be baptized, and have your special celebration then.

CHAPTER SIXTEEN
THE LONG, LONELY WINTER

TOURING THE NEIGHBORHOOD

1. How do you know when you're in the wilderness? You are lonely. Whether in fact or in feeling, no one can help, understand, or rescue you.

   A. Describe the last time you were in the wilderness of loneliness. What put you there?

   B. When you feel lonely, why does it seem no one can help, understand, or rescue you?

   C. How do you deal with times of loneliness?

2. Listen, you and I are no match for Satan. Jesus knows this. So he donned our jersey. Better still, he put on our flesh. . . . And because he did, we pass with flying colors.

   A. How do we sometimes demonstrate that we think we *are* a match for Satan? What inevitably happens?

   B. How did Jesus deal with the temptations posed by Satan?

3. Satan doesn't denounce God; he simply raises doubts about God. . . . He attempts to shift, ever so gradually, our source of confidence away from God's promise and toward our performance.

   A. How does Satan most often raise doubts about God in your life?

   B. Describe the last time your confidence started shifting away from God's promise and toward your performance. What happened?

4. Jesus' survival weapon of choice is Scripture. If the Bible was enough for his wilderness, shouldn't it be enough for ours? . . . Doubt your doubts before you doubt your beliefs.

   A. Why do you think Jesus chose Scripture as his "weapon of choice"?

   B. How do you use Scripture when you feel under spiritual attack?

   C. What does it mean to doubt your doubts before you doubt your beliefs?

CITY CENTER

1. Read Luke 4:1–13.

   A. Jesus didn't just wander into the desert; the Spirit *led* him there (v. 1). Why?

   B. When did Satan tempt Jesus with bread? When he was full or empty, strong or weak? What does this suggest about Satan's temptation of us (v. 2)?

   C. What three temptations are recorded in Scripture? How did Jesus respond to all three?

   D. What does it mean to put the Lord to the test (v. 12)?

   E. Verse 13 says Satan left Jesus "until an opportune time." What does this suggest to us about our own temptations?

2. Read James 1:13–15.

    A. What is the source of our temptations? What is *never* the source?

    B. Describe the "life cycle" of temptation and sin. Why is this life cycle important to grasp?

3. Read Hebrews 4:14–16.

    A. How does verse 14 describe the risen Christ? Why is this important to us?

    B. How does verse 15 describe Jesus? Why is this important to us?

    C. What application of these truths does verse 16 make? Have you applied the truth in this way? Explain.

COMMUNITY IMPROVEMENT

Many studies have shown that loneliness has become a national epidemic. Think about your neighbors for a moment. Who among them appears lonely? In a gentle and sensitive way, be alert to the lonely in your neighborhood, and then see what you can do to lessen that loneliness. Invite the person to join you for a game or a movie or a family outing. Try *something*. You don't have to be a doctor to help cure loneliness.

CHAPTER SEVENTEEN
GOD GETS INTO THINGS

TOURING THE NEIGHBORHOOD

1. The presence of troubles doesn't surprise us. The absence of God, however, undoes us. We can deal with the ambulance if God is in it. We can stomach the ICU if God is in it. We can face the empty house if God is in it. Is he?

    A. Describe the last time you faced a major trial. Did it feel as though God was there with you? Explain.

    B. When is it most difficult to believe that God is with you?

2. The present-tense Christ. He never says, "I was." We do. We do because "we were." We were younger, faster, prettier. Prone to be people of the past tense, we reminisce. Not God. Unwavering in

strength, he need never say, "I was." Heaven has no rearview mirrors.

A. What does it mean for us that Christ is always "present tense"?

B. Do you think God has any regrets? Explain.

3. God gets into things! Red Seas. Big fish. Lions' dens and furnaces. Bankrupt businesses and jail cells. Judean wildernesses, weddings, funerals, and Galilean tempests. Look and you'll find what everyone from Moses to Martha discovered. God in the middle of our storms. That includes yours.

A. How has God gotten into things in your life? Describe a couple of incidents.

B. How do you look for God in the middle of your personal storms?

C. How can you help others find God in the middle of their own tempests?

CITY CENTER

1. Read Matthew 14:22–33.

A. Whose idea was it for the disciples to cross to the other side of the lake (v. 22)? Why is this important to remember?

B. What did Jesus do after dismissing the crowd (v. 23)? What example does he give us?

C. Why did the disciples think Jesus was a ghost (v. 26)? How often do we mistake Jesus for something or someone else?

D. How did Jesus respond to his disciples' fear (v. 27)?

E. Do you applaud or disapprove of Peter's request (v. 28)? Why?

F. What caused Peter to sink (v. 30)? How is this very much like us?

G. How does verse 33 give an appropriate end to the story? Why would this be an appropriate end to our stories as well?

2. Read John 6:48; 8:12, 58; 10:9, 11, 36; 11:25; 14:6; 15:1.

A. Spend some time discussing each of the "I am" statements of Christ in the gospel of John. What does each one signify? How is each one meant to give you hope and a future?

B. Substitute "I was" or "I will be" for these statements. How does that affect the hope they provide?

COMMUNITY IMPROVEMENT

Teachable moments for children can be found in reaching out to those in our communities who are less fortunate. If you have children, consider taking them on a church-sponsored family missions trip to an underprivileged culture. Or you might take them to help serve for an afternoon or a day at a downtown rescue mission. Teens can help with city-sponsored literacy courses. Investigate your opportunities for service to the underprivileged, and then get the whole family involved.

CHAPTER EIGHTEEN
HOPE OR HYPE?

TOURING THE NEIGHBORHOOD

1. Ever feel as if you are walking through a religious midway?

   A. Answer this question.

   B. Describe some of the religious come-ons you've heard in the past year.

   C. How can you tell when you're hearing a religious "carnival barker"?

2. Peter's error is not that he spoke, but that he spoke heresy. Three monuments would equate Moses and Elijah with Jesus. No one shares the platform with Christ.

   A. Why shouldn't Moses and Elijah share the platform with Christ?

   B. How does Jesus far outstrip any spiritual hero of the past?

   C. Why do you think God had Moses and Elijah meet with Jesus on the mountain?

3. In the synoptic Gospels, God speaks only twice—at the baptism and then here at the Transfiguration. In both cases he begins with "This is My beloved Son." But at the river he concludes with affirmation: "in whom I am well pleased." On the hill he concludes with clarification: "Listen to Him."

A. Why do you think God spoke audibly from heaven only twice in the Gospels? Why not speak more often?

B. For what reason do you think God would say of Jesus on the first occasion, "in whom I am well pleased," while on the second he said, "Listen to Him"?

C. How do you actively listen to Jesus?

4. Make no mistake, Jesus saw himself as God. He leaves us with two options. Accept him as God, or reject him as a megalomaniac. There is no third alternative.

A. Why do you think so many people insist that Jesus never claimed to be God?

B. How would you show someone that Jesus truly did claim to be divine?

C. What decision have you made about the identity of Christ? Why did you make this decision?

CITY CENTER

1. Read Luke 9:27–36.

A. In what way was the Transfiguration a fulfillment of prophecy (v. 27)?

B. How do you think the disciples recognized Moses and Elijah (v. 33)?

C. Why do you think the disciples grew afraid as a cloud from God covered them (v. 34)?

D. Why do you think the disciples for a time kept to themselves the story of the Transfiguration (v. 36)?

2. Read Matthew 24:30.

A. What connection does this verse have with the Transfiguration story?

B. How can the truth declared by this verse give you hope and strength to continue, even in hard circumstances?

COMMUNITY IMPROVEMENT

Many religious cults claim some connection to Jesus Christ while at the same time flatly denying his divinity. Get a copy of a good resource on non-Christian cults (*Dictionary of Cults, Sects, Religions and the Occult*, for example, or Walter Martin's classic *Kingdom of the Cults*), and bone up on the reasons why Christians believe in the deity of Christ, as well as why these cultic groups deny it.

CHAPTER NINETEEN
ABANDONED!

TOURING THE NEIGHBORHOOD

1. This is a supernatural darkness. Not a casual gathering of clouds or a brief eclipse of the sun. This is a three-hour blanket of blackness.

    A. Imagine how the witnesses of this event might have reacted to the darkness.

    B. Why would God cause such a darkness?

    C. Have you experienced a sudden, dramatic act of nature? How did you react?

2. Ah, there is the hardest word. *Abandon.* The house no one wants. The child no one claims. The parent no one remembers. The Savior no one understands. He pierces the darkness with heaven's loneliest question: "My God, my God, why did you abandon me?"

    A. Describe a time when you felt abandoned.

    B. Do you ever fear being abandoned? Explain.

    C. Why would God abandon his only Son, "in whom I am well pleased"?

3. See Christ on the cross? That's a gossiper hanging there. See Jesus? Embezzler. Liar. Bigot. See the crucified carpenter? He's a wife beater. Porn addict and murderer. See Bethlehem's boy? Call him by his other names—Adolf Hitler, Osama bin Laden, and Jeffrey Dahmer.

A. Was it unfair of God to place the sin of the world on his perfectly obedient Son? Explain.

B. Does Jesus' hesitation in the Garden of Gethsemane make more sense to you when you ponder the sin he "became" on the cross? Explain.

CITY CENTER

1. Read Matthew 27:45–54.

   A. Why do you think Matthew tells us about the darkness that covered the land for three hours (v. 45)?

   B. What do you think was going through Jesus' mind as he cried out the words recorded in verse 46?

   C. What happened at the moment that Jesus died (vv. 51–53)? Why are these things significant?

   D. How did the Roman soldiers react to what they saw (v. 54)?

2. Read Psalm 22:1–18.

   A. Read carefully through these verses, and see how many prophetic fulfillments you can find in the crucifixion of Christ.

   B. When you are fearful, what scripture gives you strength?

3. Read 2 Timothy 4:9–18.

   A. Briefly describe Paul's personal situation as he speaks of it in this passage.

   B. How did the apostle react to being abandoned (vv. 10, 16)?

   C. How did the apostle find strength in God even in his abandonment (vv. 17–18)? How can we do the same?

COMMUNITY IMPROVEMENT

A popular worship song says Jesus was abandoned so we didn't have to be. But some people—including Christians—feel abandoned nonetheless. You can help break the chains of abandonment by demonstrating your care and concern for someone in your world. From a small beginning, such as an invitation to dinner, you can show someone that he or she has not been abandoned. If a personal invitation might be overwhelming to the person, try a group event, such as a neighborhood party. Call it a "get-acquainted" party, implying that there will be others in the group who are new to the neighborhood, thereby making the event more welcoming and less intimidating.

CHAPTER TWENTY
CHRIST'S *COUP DE GRÂCE*

TOURING THE NEIGHBORHOOD

1. Don't we howl? Not at car washes perhaps but at hospital stays and job transfers. Let the economy go south or the kids move north, and we have a wail of a time. And when our Master explains what's happening, we react as if he's speaking Yalunka. We don't understand a word he says.

    A. How do you normally react when unexpected difficulties hit? Do you wail? Explain.

    B. Describe a time when you just couldn't understand what God was doing in your life. In hindsight, what do you now think God might have been doing?

    C. Is your present world "wet and wild"? Explain. What have you learned that can help you weather this time?

2. More Old Testament foretellings were realized during the crucifixion than on any other day. Twenty-nine different prophecies, the youngest of which was five hundred years old, were completed on the day of Christ's death.

    A. Does it encourage you or inspire you in your faith to realize how many ancient prophecies Christ fulfilled while on the cross? Why or why not?

    B. Have you ever done a study on fulfilled prophecy? If not, why not?

3. Don't call Jesus a victim of circumstances. Call him an orchestrator of circumstances! He engineered the action of his enemies to fulfill prophecy. And he commandeered the tongues of his enemies to declare truth.

A. Think through the gospel story. How did God appear to arrange circumstances to orchestrate the result he desired?

B. If God really does orchestrate even what appear to be tragic circumstances for the benefit of his people, how should that affect the way you live? Does it so affect your life? Explain.

4. I dare you to find one element of the cross that he did not manage for good or recycle for symbolism. Give it a go. I think you'll find what I found—every dark detail was actually a golden moment in the cause of Christ.

A. Take Max's challenge. What do you discover?

B. How do you think God can take "every dark detail" of your own life and use it for your ultimate good?

CITY CENTER

1. Read Matthew 26:24, 31, 54, 56; John 12:20–27; 13:18; 17:12.

A. What do all of these texts have in common?

B. Why is it important for us to realize that Jesus knew exactly what was happening as the time of his arrest drew near?

C. What confidence can it give you in your faith to realize that God has history under control?

2. Read John 11:49–52.

A. Who spoke prophetically in this passage (v. 49)? Why is that unusual?

B. What do you think the speaker meant to convey through his statement? What did God intend for his words to convey (vv. 51–52)?

C. How does this incident demonstrate God's shepherding of history— yours included?

3. Read Acts 4:23–31.

A. How did their knowledge of prophecy frame the apostles' interpretation of Jesus' crucifixion?

B. Did the fulfillment of prophecy encourage the apostles or make them fearful? What did they do as a result?

COMMUNITY IMPROVEMENT

If you'd like a gripping, journalistic-style account of what happened when Jesus went to the cross, get a copy of Jim Bishop's *The Day Christ Died*. Bishop uses modern reportorial techniques and up-to-date historical information to paint a fascinating picture of what happened on the day Jesus gave his life for humankind.

CHAPTER TWENTY-ONE
CHRIST'S CRAZY CLAIM

TOURING THE NEIGHBORHOOD

1. An occupied tomb on Sunday takes the good out of Good Friday.

   A. Why would an occupied tomb on Sunday take the good out of Good Friday?

   B. What was good about the death of Christ? Why couldn't the disciples see this ahead of time?

2. The empty tomb never resists honest investigation. A lobotomy is not a prerequisite of discipleship. Following Christ demands faith, but not blind faith.

   A. How is it possible to investigate the Crucifixion and Resurrection two millenniums after the Gospels say they occurred?

   B. Give some examples of intelligent questions regarding the truth of Christianity.

   C. What is the difference between faith and blind faith? Why is one legitimate and the other not?

3. The courage of these men and women was forged in the fire of the empty tomb. The disciples did not dream up a resurrection. The Resurrection fired up the disciples. Have doubts about the empty tomb? Come and see the disciples.

   A. Compare the actions and demeanor of the disciples before and after Resurrection Sunday. What differences do you note?

   B. Why is it harder to believe that the disciples dreamed up the Resurrection than that the Resurrection fired up the disciples?

4. Just like passengers in the airport about to board a plane, we get to choose how we respond. Either board and trust the pilot—or try to get home on our own.

   A. How do some people try to get home on their own?

   B. How do you demonstrate your trust in the "Pilot"? Could observers see this trust? Explain.

CITY CENTER

1. Read Matthew 28:1–10.

   A. To whom did the angel direct his comments in this passage (v. 5)? Why do you think he didn't speak to the guards?

   B. What did the angel tell the women? What did he direct them to do (vv. 5–7)?

   C. Why do you think the women were both afraid and filled with joy at the angel's words (v. 8)?

   D. Why do you think the risen Christ would tell his disciples to go to Galilee, where he would appear to them? Why not appear to them where they already were?

2. Read Acts 2:22–41.

   A. How does Peter begin his comments on Jesus in this passage (v. 22)? Why start out this way?

   B. How does Peter interpret the arrest and crucifixion of Christ (v. 23)?

   C. What event does Peter highlight in his sermon (vv. 24–32)?

   D. How does Peter connect this event to what has just happened in Jerusalem (v. 33)?

   E. What conclusion does Peter state in verse 36?

   F. What solution does Peter suggest in verses 38–40?

3. Read 1 Corinthians 15:1–8, 12–20.

   A. Name the main points of the "gospel" Paul said he preached.

   B. What personal connection did the apostle have to these events (v. 8)?

   C. Why is the resurrection of Christ central to the message of Christianity (vv. 12–20)? What happens without it?

COMMUNITY IMPROVEMENT

The resurrection of Jesus Christ forms the cornerstone of our entire faith—but that cornerstone does people no good if they don't know about it. When was the last time you told someone else about the great Savior you have? Who in your sphere of influence still needs to hear about Jesus? Make a list of the five people in your life who first come to mind. Commit to praying for them, that they might invite Jesus to become their Savior—and pray specifically for how you might fit into the introduction.

CONCLUSION
STILL IN THE NEIGHBORHOOD

TOURING THE NEIGHBORHOOD

1. Why the immensity? Why such vast, unmeasured, unexplored, "unused" space? So that you and I, freshly stunned, could be stirred by this resolve: "I can do all things through Christ who strengthens me."

   A. How does the vastness of space make you feel? Awed? Miniscule? Explain.

   B. How does the immensity of space encourage us to believe that we can do all things through Christ, who strengthens us?

2. The Christ of the galaxies is the Christ of your Mondays. The Starmaker manages your travel schedule. Relax. You have a friend in high places.

   A. Does knowing that Christ both runs the universe and watches over you help you to relax? Explain.

   B. How close are you to your friend Jesus? Could you call him a best friend? Why or why not?

3. Even in heaven, Christ remains our next door Savior. Even in heaven, he is still "Christ Jesus . . . who died." The King of the universe commands comets with a human tongue and directs celestial traffic with a human hand. Still human. Still divine. Living forever through his two natures.

A. Why is it important for us to remember that Jesus forever remains both human and divine?

B. Do you look forward to shaking the very real hand of your very real Savior? Explain.

4. Even though he is in heaven, he never left the neighborhood.

A. How could Jesus be both in heaven and in your neighborhood?

B. Does it help you to think of Jesus as a next door Savior? Explain.

CITY CENTER

1. Read Romans 8:34.

A. What current role does this verse assign to Jesus Christ?

B. How does this role encourage you to keep moving ahead in your faith?

2. Read Ephesians 1:15–23.

A. What requests did Paul make of God on behalf of the Ephesians (vv. 17–19)?

B. What do you learn about Christ's resurrection (vv. 19–20)?

C. What do you learn about Christ's current activities (vv. 20–22)?

D. How do these truths affect you?

3. Read Matthew 28:16–20.

A. Why do you think that when the disciples saw Jesus after his resurrection, most worshiped him but some doubted (v. 17). What was there to doubt?

B. How did Jesus describe his status in verse 18? What significance does this have for us?

C. What commands does Jesus give his disciples in verses 19–20? How are you complying with these directions?

D. What promise does Jesus give in verse 20? How is this designed to encourage and strengthen us?

COMMUNITY IMPROVEMENT

Spend some time in prayer thanking God for sending his Son, Jesus Christ, to be your next door Savior. Thank him for the specific benefits he has granted you. Praise him for his kindness in providing such a wonderful Savior. And ask him how you might be able to share your Savior's love with others, whether under your own roof or in your own neighborhood.

Notes

Chapter 2: Christ's Theme Song

1. Jeordan Legon, "From Science and Computers, a New Face of Jesus," 25 December 2002. Found at www.cnn.com/2002/TECH/science/12/25/face.jesus.

2. Dean Farrar, *The Life of Christ* (London, England: Cassell & Company, Ltd., n.d.), 84.

Chapter 3: Friend of Flops

1. Thanks to Landon Saunders for sharing this story with me.

Chapter 6: Spit Therapy

1. Joni Eareckson Tada et al., *When Morning Gilds the Skies: Hymns of Heaven and Our Eternal Hope* (Wheaton, Ill.: Crossway Books, 2002), 23–24. Used by permission.

Chapter 7: What Jesus Says at Funerals

1. Used by permission of Karen and Bill Davis.

2. Billy Sprague, *Letter to a Grieving Heart: Comfort and Hope for Those Who Hurt* (Eugene, Oreg.: Harvest House, 2001), 9.

Chapter 8: Getting the Hell Out

1. Not her real name.

2. Linda Dillow and Lorraine Pintus, *Gift-Wrapped by God: Secret Answers to the Question, "Why Wait?"* (Colorado Springs, Colo.: WaterBrook Press, 2002), 59–64. Used by permission.

Chapter 9: It's Not Up to You

1. John MacArthur, Jr., *The MacArthur New Testament Commentary: Matthew 8–15* (Chicago: Moody Press, 1987), 281–283.

Part Two: No Place He Won't Go

1. Paul Aurandt, *Destiny and 102 Other Real-Life Mysteries* (New York: Bantam Books, 1983), 225.

Chapter 11: He Loves to Be with the Ones He Loves

1. Maxie Dunnam, *This Is Christianity* (Nashville: Abingdon Press, 1994), 60–61.

Chapter 13: A Cure for the Common Life

1. Dean Farrar, *The Life of Christ* (London: Cassell and Co., Ltd., 1906), 57.

2. George Connor, comp., *Listening to Your Life: Daily Meditations with Frederick Buechner* (San Francisco: Harper & Row Publishers, 1992), 2.

3. Destiny went to be with Jesus on December 3, 2002.

Chapter 14: Oh, to Be DTP-Free!

1. Taken from Don Stephens, "Of Mercy—and Peanut Butter," The Mercy Minute, at www.mercyships.org/mercyminute/vol5/mmv5-32.htm, and Harold S. McNabb Jr., "Inspirational Thoughts from the Legacy of George Washington Carver," speech at Iowa State University.

2. Psalm 119:18 KJV.

Chapter 15: Tire Kicker to Car Buyer

1. My thanks to Bob Russell for sharing this story.

Chapter 17: God Gets into Things

1. Ann Coulter, "Dressing for Distress," 24 October 2001. Found at www.worldnetdaily.com.

2. Frederick Dale Bruner, *The Churchbook: Matthew 13–28*, vol. 2 of *Matthew: A Commentary by Frederick Dale Bruner* (Dallas: Word Publishing, 1990), 534.

Chapter 18: Hope or Hype?

1. "Chosen" is the translation of *agapetos*, "the absolutely unique and solitary one." "Son" is preceded by a definite article: "*the* Son of mine," *ho huios mou.* Ibid., 606.

2. C. S. Lewis, *Mere Christianity* (New York: MacMillan, 1952), 56.

Chapter 19: Abandoned!

1. Matthew Henry, *Matthew to John*, vol. 5 of *Matthew Henry's Commentary on the Whole Bible* (Old Tappan, N.J.: Fleming H. Revell Company, 1985), 428.

2. Walter Bauer, *A Greek-English Lexicon of the New Testament*, trans. William F. Arndt and F. Wilbur Gingrich (Chicago: University of Chicago Press, 1979), 50.

Chapter 20: Christ's Coup de Grâce

1. Josh McDowell, *The New Evidence That Demands a Verdict* (Nashville: Thomas Nelson, 1999), 193.

2. Ibid., 186, 189, 192.

Chapter 21: Christ's Crazy Claim

1. Peter Lewis, *The Glory of Christ* (London, England: Hodder & Stoughton, 1992), 342.

Conclusion: Still in the Neighborhood

1. John Piper, *Seeing and Savoring Jesus Christ* (Wheaton, Ill.: Crossway Books, 2001), 19.

2. John MacArthur, Jr., *The MacArthur New Testament Commentary: Colossians and Philemon* (Chicago: Moody Press, 1992), 48.

3. Piper, *Seeing and Savoring Jesus Christ,* 19.

4. MacArthur, Jr., *MacArthur New Testament Commentary: Colossians and Philemon,* 47.

5. Lewis, *Glory of Christ,* 135.

6. Charles J. Rolls, *Time's Noblest Name: The Names and Titles of Jesus Christ* (Neptune, N.J.: Loizeaux Brothers, 1985), 84–86.

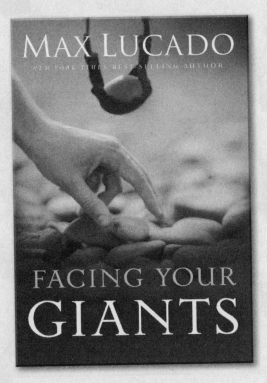

The Teaching Ministry of Max Lucado

UpWords brings to radio and the Internet a message of hope, pure and simple, in Jesus Christ!

Visit www.MaxLucado.com to find FREE valuable resources for spiritual growth and encouragement, such as:

- Archives of UpWords, Max's daily radio program. You will also find a listing of radio stations and broadcast times in your area.
- Daily devotionals
- Book excerpts
- Exclusive features and presentations
- Subscription information on how you can receive e-mail messages from Max
- Downloads of audio, video, and printed material
- Ways to receive mobile content

You will also find an online store and special offers.

www.MaxLucado.com

1-800-822-9673

UpWords Ministries
P.O. Box 692170
San Antonio, TX 78269-2170

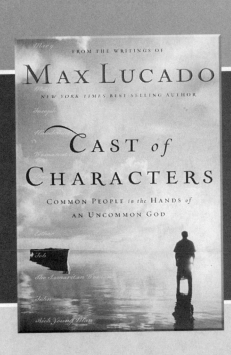

These classic Bible character stories are a great invitation into the heartland of God's Word.

Some of the most powerful stories from the Bible will come alive for today's readers through these inspiring selections from the writings of Max Lucado. Max provides a compelling look at the most high-impact moments in the biblical narrative, drawn from his previous twenty-plus years of writing.

At the end of each chapter will be study guide questions so the reader can go deeper.

Extraordinary stories are told about the following characters:

Mary, Peter, Matthew, Joseph, Nicodemus, Woman at the Well, David, Esther, Job, The Samaritan Woman, John, Rich Young Man.

And more . . .

The Bestseller Collection

These affordable, yet high-quality hardcover books are priced for sharing the timeless and timely messages of Max Lucado. Share them with friends, family, and coworkers, or perhaps introduce a fan to a volume previously missed, or connect Max's amazing messages of grace with someone brand new.

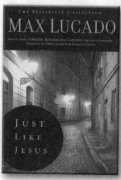
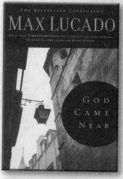
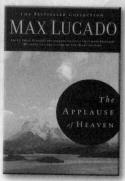
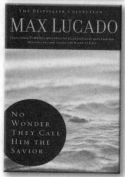
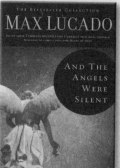
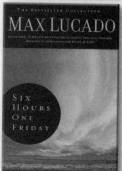

Entire Collection Available Now

# of Max Lucado

Join us as we collect these jewels from the treasure box of Max's timeless bestsellers for a fitting display of insight and inspiration.

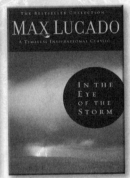
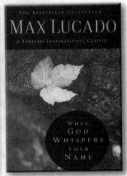

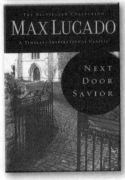
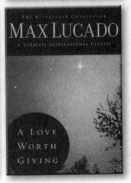
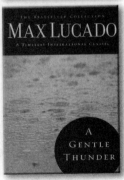

For more information, visit:

www.MaxLucado.com · www.ThomasNelson.com

If 9/11 are the numbers of terror and despair, then 3:16 are the numbers of hope.

MAX LUCADO

NEW YORK TIMES BEST–SELLING AUTHOR

...ING AUTHOR

Available Summer 2009

3:16

THE NUMBERS OF HOPE

Best-selling author Max Lucado leads readers through a word-by-word study of John 3:16, the passage that he calls the "Hope Diamond" of Scripture.

PREMIER LIBRARY EDITIONS
from Max Lucado

These beautiful hardcovers have been chosen, not only for their best-selling status but for their unique place in the body of Max's work. They are paradigm shifters, movement makers, and deserve special recognition as works that have had significant impact on the Church.

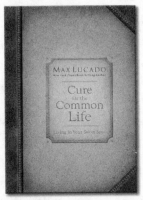

Cure for the Common Life

He Chose the Nails

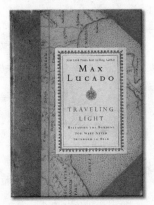

Traveling Light

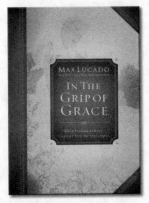

In the Grip of Grace

For more information, visit
www.MaxLucado.com or *www.ThomasNelson.com*

FEARLESS CARDS AND GIFTS FROM DAYSPRING

Touch someone's life and bring encouragement to their day with a Max Lucado greeting card or gift from DaySpring.

The Max Lucado line from DaySpring includes a large variety of products, including greeting cards, journals, coffee mugs, and more.

SHARE YOUR HEART AND GOD'S LOVE
www.dayspring.com

Find them today at a local Christian bookstore near you.

Fearless Worship is the companion CD to *Fearless* from Max Lucado. The album features the well known voices and songs in worship music today. Big Daddy Weave, Travis Cottrell, Lenny LeBlanc, Cindy Morgan, Nicole C Mullen and many more join voices with Max Lucado in walking a life free from fear . . . a life abandoned to the One who will shoulder it all. From Morgan's majestic "Praise the King" to the surrender of Mullen's "On My Knees," *Fearless Worship* will lead you into his presence where you will begin to trust more and fear less!

For more information visit www.fearlessworship.com

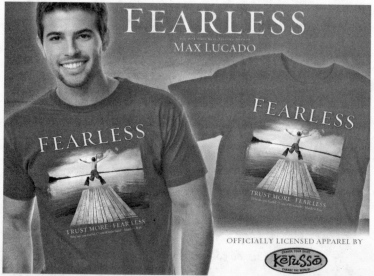

OFFICIALLY LICENSED APPAREL BY